Not to Spoil the Ending...

...but everything is going to be ok

Not to Spoil the Ending...

...but everything is going to be ok

Insights from a
teenager in Heaven
about Happiness here

Naomi Brickel

ADAMSWORLD

Published by AdamsWorld LLC

First paperback edition August 2021

Book design by Alejandro Martin
Edited by Hannah Howard and Elaine Porter

The events, conversations, and written communications have been set down to the best of the author's ability, although some details have been changed to protect the privacy of individuals. Every effort has been made to trace or contact all copyright holders. The publishers will be pleased to make good any omissions or rectify any mistakes brought to their attention at the earliest opportunity.

ISBN 978-1-7374204-0-8 (paperback)
ISBN 978-1-7374204-1-5 (ebook)

www.naomibrickel.com

To Doug,

If they'd shown either of us a movie trailer about
our life when we met, we would've both run. I'm
glad we didn't. Thanks for your easy way. We
done good.

RILY.

Contents:

Climax

Darkness

Flashlights

Climax

Chapter 2 - Where's Adam?

Sunday, November 12, 2017
11pm
Home

"Mom... Hey. Mom, wake up... Have you seen Adam?" It was JohnPaul, Adam's 18-year-old older brother. Adam was 15. He was the fifth child in my large family, and one of 4 boys. Adam and Johnny (as most of his friends and siblings called him) had grown very close over those last three months. Johnny was in the first semester of a gap year, and had not gone off to college with his classmates, who had graduated the previous June. He was attending our local community college part time and had agreed to be the "mannie" for his two little brothers to help pay for his classes. He'd taken on the roles of Adam's chauffeur, servant, and best friend.

Now Johnny was standing in my bedroom doorway, concerned - not frantic or agitated - wondering where Adam could be. He spoke as he woke me. I was asleep with the light still on. I must have fallen asleep reading.

It seems only fitting to begin with a "Chapter 2," in a section within the "Climax," in a book where the title gives away the ending. As a former English major, I know that literature should not happen this way, but in the general manner I live, I'm beginning a bit undisciplined. It fits, because what transpired over the next several hours diminishes everything prior. Don't get me wrong, life before was rich and meaningful. I grew up in a family of seven, birthed six kids of my own, and lived an existence anyone would note to be full of WTF mile-marking events, intrigue, and drama - enough before this moment to fill chapters. But things were about to be forever altered. Going forward, my life and the lives of all my family would be marked indelibly right here. Unknown to any of us, this moment would come to delineate a clearly defined before and after.

"Mom, where's Adam?" Johnny asked again, both of us were unaware of the gravity, that this would become THE question, initiating a course of events that would change all of us. This moment would become a dramatic reset in our lives and, as I learned, the lives of many others. Definitely a climax.

I don't remember where Doug was. He might have been in the bathroom reading. Strangely, I barely recall my husband's part in that night's drama. Battling the progression of Parkinson's disease for the prior six years, he was no longer able to work due to his advanced physical and cognitive symptoms. And his personality had changed; a strong, manly, friendly, laid back, and easy guy had become forgetful, incapacitated, confused, negative and accusing. Now, he often assumed the worst of the kids or me in a given situation, which, of course, compromised tranquility in a house of teenagers and young adults. Sadly, with the progressing manifestation of his illness, he had lost relevance and command in the eyes of his kids. So, when JohnPaul came in, he was looking for me.

"Mom!"

Yes. This life-altering moment punctuated a cloud that had developed over our home and family, already in the midst of trying years, already in mourning. My memories of earlier that afternoon are vivid. While out for a walk just hours earlier, I had stopped into the church where I grew up. With tear-filled eyes and my heart full of despair over how sad and difficult life had become, I sought consolation. I was at the end of my rope, seeing his visible decline, frightened about where it was leading, anxious about my kids and how I would be able to manage the house, teenager issues, problems, fear of the future, job pressure, and all of it alone without a partner. The kids were also suffering over Doug's decline. We had recently dealt with many issues related to their conflicted emotions and mine. I begged God to lighten things. What an ironic response He would offer; I still shake my head. Certainly, this couldn't be expected on top of it all.

"Huh? What? What do you mean 'Where's Adam?' Johnny?? No. It's late. I'm asleep. He should be too. I would assume he's in bed. Did you look?" I was irritable, groggy. It was a Sunday night, late, too late for Adam to be out, too late for me to need to deal with the hassle of teenagers. I had work in the morning. There was school tomorrow. I was responsible for so much, why did they need to add to it all with things like this? "He should be asleep. ('G-d damn it!'" under my breath.)

"No. He's not in bed. Mom, I think you should get up." It was strange, yes, but I couldn't imagine any need for worry. Why was Johnny uneasy? My teenage boys, being typical, seemed to lack good judgement. Questions like, "Where's Adam?" on a Sunday night were more exasperating than worrisome. I proceeded to get up, feeling weary, resigned and annoyed. I had gone to bed earlier than usual, depressed and

5

lonely. After my discouraging day, I had taken something to help me sleep. I rarely did that and recall as the concern began to surface, feeling anxious about being compromised in my ability to be alert. It was an unnecessary worry. The adrenaline which would pour into me shortly would do more than bring me to my full senses.

"Johnny, where is he? When was the last time you talked to him??" I asked with exasperation.

"Mom, I was in bed. We were talking on our phones. He went to walk Kelly (our dog), but I think it's been awhile. I must have fallen asleep. He should have been back by now," he responded. "I think you need to come down."

I got up and we went downstairs to the kitchen. As we descended the stairs I began to feel anxious. By the time I was in the kitchen, I felt a slowly rising sense of crisis. Fear kicked in quickly.

"Johnny! How long has it been!? We need to go out and find him!" Foreboding filled me. I envisioned all the bad things that could be happening to him. Anxiously, deliberately, even angrily, I went to our deck door to call out into the yard for him. I pulled the sliding door open, purposefully and forcefully, to yell out to him in the night.

In that split second, my hand still on the door, looking out, ready to yell out to him, my worst fears were provoked. As I slid the door open into an opaque darkness, Kelly was there right in front of me, waiting. Crying, her leash dangling, frantic, excited, she was jumping around our deck, almost begging for help. Kelly is a smart, noble and amazing mixed Border Collie rescue mutt, loyal, loving, patient, protective and gentle with her rough and sometimes neglectful masters. She was agitated. I knew she would never have left Adam. And I knew Adam would not have left her out here. He loved Kelly, never forgot to walk her, and would not just leave her on a whim. Nothing could account for her here without him, no explanation. My instincts screamed, knowing it was bad.

"Kelly! Where is he?!? Kelly, where's Adam!!?? Kelly! Bring me to Adam!" I begged. She continued to bark and spin, worked up. I ran down and into the yard imploring her to take me to him. She frantically jumped at me and barked, but did not lead me anywhere. Oh my God, this was really bad. I was panicked. How long had she been there waiting for us to come help her? How long had he been gone?

I knew he must be in great danger. Or gone. I thought of him kidnapped, beaten up, stuffed in the trunk of a car. How far away was he? How could I stop him from being taken? I was sick at the thought of my child (even if he had recently grown manly) in the hands of bad people, being harmed. I could feel his fear and my own sense of helplessness in a way I'd never experienced.

Oh my God! Johnny, we need to call 911!" I ran back into the house to the phone, "Johnny, you have to go look for him!!" He ran out into the night. I remember feeling an ache, knowing I was sending my teenage child out with a greater responsibility than most grown men will ever be burdened with … I called 911.

I don't recall my words, but know that I was relaying the fears of a parent whose child is missing (but not lying dead a half a block away) frantic that he might be in the hands of someone evil, being driven further from me even as I tried to report the details of his last sighting, panic-stricken and powerless. Hysteria over his safety overtook me. I knew that I was in the midst of the worst thing that would ever happen. Still, I never imagined his lifeless body lying a few hundred feet away on the cold sidewalk. I never fathomed he could be dead nearby. As I relayed details to the operator, I willed myself to remain in control as I spoke.

"ADAM!!!! NO ADAAAAAAAAM!! NOOOOOOOO! ADAAAAAAAM!!!"

As I continued to communicate details to the operator, JohnPaul's blood-curdling screams pierced the controlled process I was taking efforts to maintain. I screamed into the phone that he was found and it was bad, and that I needed to go to him. I don't know if I finished the call or just dropped the phone. I ran, through the yards and into the front yard of our neighbors whose house faced the other street.

There he was, lying on the grass next to the road, half under a car. I don't remember anything about the car or whose it turned out to be; where he must have tried to rest for support as he breathed his last breaths; where he must have leaned, knowing something was wrong; where he must have stopped, and perhaps experienced the sudden possible fear of his life ending, even the actual knowledge it was.

There he was, lifeless ... but I still did not process, dead.

JohnPaul was over him, powerfully pumping his chest. He had pulled him from the road onto the grass. He is perhaps the most courageous person I have ever known. After all of it, I guess all my kids are, and they have each shown it in such different ways. In that moment of crisis though, he was the one in charge as I looked on in shock. He knew what he needed to do. He acted. I wonder if I would have been paralyzed had I gotten there first.

I went in close to look, and then pulled back to make room and be out of the way. Adam's mouth was full of his own vomit. He was greyish purple. His eyes were open, and I think I wrongly deduced that meant he was still here, weakened, but still with us. I don't recall wondering or thinking about whether or not his heart was beating. I do remember that I continued to think it was foul play, that he had been assaulted. I envisioned gruesome men. I pictured my precious son being battered and unable to protect himself. I thought he must have been knocked out, that the back of his head might be crushed in, and I was scared for anyone to roll him over. But why? Were there bad people roaming my neighborhood? Were they watching us right now, laughing? Had he gotten in trouble? Or was he in with some sort of drug crowd, messed up with the wrong people? I was confused and angry at Kelly for not protecting him, for running, for leaving him to be hurt by dangerous people who had invaded our peace.

Amy and Rich, our next-door neighbors and lifelong friends, came out. Their kids align with ours in age and friendship, and their son Tommy is Adam's age. Tommy and Adam were best friends before they could walk, or either of them remembered.

Kirsty and Ged from across the street, who also had kids close to mine, were there. Their daughter, Lili Mae, was one of the first on the scene after JohnPaul. She took over the CPR for Johnny, pumping and pumping, calling Adam back. She, too, was one of Adam's first and lifelong friends. As toddlers, in their separate houses, they used to get up on chairs so they could see each other through the windows across the street. They would talk forever on the phone as they looked over at one another, and would share frosting on cupcakes and everything else important. I had pictures of them sharing spoons and cake so comfortably at birthdays. It all seemed like yesterday, and now this! Lili Mae was just 15 years old, but calm and adultlike, trying to bring him back, without agitation or emotion, reassuring Adam he was going to be okay, coaxing him to come back to us with a positive, prodding, encouragement. She, Ged, and Rich took turns with JohnPaul, pushing hard on Adam's chest, urging him back.

I stayed back and let them all work. Sitting down on the grass nearby, out of everyone's way, I watched and realized I was not in control. I didn't know if he was alive or dead, and I didn't consider it. Everything emotional stopped inside me. I was ice, or like a computer, outside of the situation, a spectator, calm.

The police and firemen arrived as Ged was pumping. They seemed to stand by and observe but not really enter into the action or take command. Ged looked up at one point and asked them if they would take over, but I don't understand or remember the details explaining why they didn't. They asked questions. I perceived an assumption he might have overdosed on drugs. I still feel my defensiveness, and admittedly, a simultaneous vulnerable fear and confusion that it might somehow, inexplicably, be the case. They did not know my good and level son - or was it me?

I never thought of or considered, his heart. Adam had a condition called hypertrophic cardiomyopathy, HCM. But this was never supposed to happen. I told a cop about the diagnosis because he asked of any underlying conditions. As I shared, I thought the information would be helpful if he needed testing or surgery, or so that they would not be confused by strange EKG or test results as they treated him in the hospital, just so they would not be distracted from whatever it was that was real. His was the type of condition that took the lives of people who never knew they had it, not my kids. I had prepared and it was in control; I had researched and knew everything there was to know. He went to the best specialists in NYC every year. To be safe, he did not play sports. We had taken all the right precautions.

In fact, the last time we had been to his doctor, almost exactly one year prior, they were confident it might never impact him. This was definitely not part of the plan and never even entered my mind. Even after, when the doctor in the hospital confirmed that Adam had died because of an arrhythmia due to his HCM, I doubted. "Who is this ER non-specialist?" In hindsight it still puzzles me that I never thought of it as I looked on, unemotional and paralyzed, as JohnPaul and Lili Mae tried to coax Adam back, encouraging breaths to be taken, begging his silent heart to beat.

In the midst of it all, I noticed our neighbor Ali, a younger mom from several houses up the street, come out and look. Ali had lost her 3-year-old son of a horrible and random respiratory illness a few years earlier. I saw Kirsty go over to her and say something I couldn't hear, and she turned around and went in. She had wanted to know who it was, and was told it was Adam, it was not good, and she should go back inside. It would be too difficult for her to have to experience. I remember feeling alarmed and upset that she had to see it all happening, thinking how pained she must be. I remained outside myself, an objective observer, aware of her trauma but somehow distant from my own. I did not process that what was transpiring in front of me would bond us.

I remember so many of the details. It's incredible to me how my mind could process the chaos, registering all the particulars of everything happening instantaneously, yet I never once contemplated the obvious outcome.

After what seemed like a long time, though it could have been seconds, or a few or many minutes, I got up from the grass and went calmly to each police officer and fireman, inquiring if Adam had a pulse. They were avoidant, not wanting to engage or make eye contact. I couldn't get an answer. I became frustrated, but remained outwardly calm and controlled, desperate enough for answers to repress any feelings of irritation and resentment that might get between us and my needed clarity. At some point an ambulance and EMTs arrived and got into the action. I watched as they employed some sort of mechanical pumping machine to continue the work his brother, friends, and neighbors were losing the energy to continue. Still, no one touched him or attempted to revive. I think back now and wonder if my memory is inaccurate, or if they just knew more than I did. He was lifted onto a stretcher and into the ambulance, the machine pumping his chest. I expected I would have to go with him, but they told us we couldn't. Something was explained for this, and JohnPaul and I were directed to a police car. I don't know what we talked about. I can't imagine what we would have had to say, or the terrible experience it must have been for the officer who drove us. It was surreal, these initial moments, a detached experience of the reality that would shroud the rest of my life.

Chaos and Control

Ten minutes later I was walking through the automatic doors into the Emergency Room of our local hospital. The atmosphere, all the sights and sounds as I walked through, was redolent of a night fourteen years earlier, when I had frantically stormed through the same doors, with my child's limp lifeless body in my arms. I remembered it clearly all those years before, shouting at the hospital staff that he was not breathing; imploring, screaming and demanding help. Sometime around a year old, barely a toddler, Adam had also brushed death. The details of that night were vivid, and I noted (and now feel the irony) that I entered much more cold and calmly now. It is curious that this time I was less agitated and distressed, contained enough in this crisis to remember the original one.

The hospital was strange and incongruous. Adam was rushed into the ER and quickly into one of the rooms, rather than a curtained cubicle. JohnPaul and I were directed to chairs facing an older patient in his cubicle bed, about as far away as we could physically be from him while still remaining in the ER. The patient in the bed and the woman accompanying him looked at us. There was nowhere else to direct their eyes. What strange places emergency rooms are, the way people are thrust into each other's moments of crisis, maintaining some sort of anonymity, but without the dignity of any privacy. How unnatural it must

13

have felt for them, looking at the mom and brother of the frenzied crisis that had gone past minutes before. Did they know? What was in their heads as they silently stared?

We sat there waiting. I felt closer to JohnPaul than I had ever felt to him before, even as my child, because the connection was suddenly much more like one between adults, peers. A new and unique bond, generated from the intensity of it all, was already present in those first stunned moments. It would develop further through the conversations, shared recollections, therapy, tears and trauma, and an eventual trip to a tattoo shop in Maine, with an intense bonding collaboration in our developed designs representing our shared experience.

It was no surprise seeing him there so calm and self-possessed. He had always been a tough no drama kid. Fierce and fearless, he was described once by his youth football coach as having more strength per ounce than other players. "He takes out kids twice his size," and "sends them flying when he makes contact." Johnny liked to climb trees past safe heights, and do backflips from a standing position on the lawn. He might beat up an older kid on the bus who teased his sister with autism, but in his protectiveness, he was "no fuss" and would instruct her sternly after, showing her how to be smarter with the mean kids. As I sat there, I was also aware of his sensitivity, which had become more apparent with his dad's declining health. With Billy (the oldest) away at college, I had watched him take on a more "man of the house" role, especially when it came to Jude, 11, his youngest brother. He recognized that Jude did not have the benefit of growing up with a dad in the same way he had, and made time every day for the trampoline, a football or lacrosse catch in the yard, or just something fun and fatherly with him.

As we sat there I became restive, stuck on the periphery, uncontrollably disengaged from what was happening and feeling helpless to become so, with my mind racing about how I could change it. I felt an urgency to force myself into things but did not want to upset Johnny by acting overwrought or pushy. This distanced phenomenon is not unusual in emergency rooms (with six kids I've spent a lot of time there), with staff at desks in the middle of it all, but separated completely, focused on their tasks at hand on work that the loved ones do not play into. It is awkward to get their attention, to attempt to acquire answers or information knowing that what they are focused on might be more critical for someone else's life or death than your need for information. The disconnection frustrated me, and I couldn't fight the need to get up and ensure they knew I was there.

Amy and Kirsty, who had been there on the street, had gotten right in a car, followed behind us, and came in. It provided a sense of relief. No longer alone, I felt alleviated of some of the pressure to experience this the right way and make good decisions. My memory of the details gets cloudier after this. Perhaps the comfort of their presence let me take a breath, and in doing so my mind stopped recording the nightmare.

At some point the doctor came to me. How difficult it had to be for him, knowing what he knew and I still didn't. The machine was still on, pumping aggressively at Adam's poor body. I can't recall what he was prepared to tell me, or what he shared unprompted, though I remember interrogating him for the information I needed.

"Do you have an idea of how long he has not had a pulse?"

"Has he had any heart beat since he got here?"

"Did he have a pulse at any time on the scene or in the ambulance?" ... calculating time in my head ... continuing ...

"Is there any kind of chance that he could be ok, like a functioning person with any kind of life, if you could get him back now?"

His sobering answer.

Surrounded in ER chaos, I was totally alone with a decision to be made in an instant. No chance to process, deliberate, weigh, confer. The most exigent grave choice that I suspect (and strongly hope) I will ever confront. An awful burden, but in some strange way empowering, for a mother who endures the process of such a decision is never the same; she's either broken or stronger. She finds the perseverance, endurance and hope needed to survive, or she dies inside with the child she lets go.

I responded calmly, "Ok. Yes. I want to see him. But first please go turn off that machine."

Adam was dead.

Two and a Half Years Later

June 25, 2020
New Rochelle High School
Class of 2020 Graduation
via Zoom

Mr. Joseph Starvaggi, Principal:

*"It is also now my pleasure and my honor to present an award
to the family of Adam Brickel. Adam was a light to his peers and a
beacon of hope to many. He loved life in the purest and simplest of ways.
Whether Adam was playing a stunt on his sisters, catching up with his
teachers on the latest episode of 'The Walking Dead,' walking his family
dog, or simply enjoying a New Ro game, Adam loved life in the simplest
of ways, and his love was pure.*

*"Although quiet, he attracted friends from all socioeconomic
and ethnic groups. Although not a member of a sports team, he attended
every game. His life was a testament to what it means to be 'New Ro
Strong.' His quiet strength became a galvanizing force.*

*"Adam is gone, but certainly not forgotten. I will present this
award to his family, and ask his mom, Naomi Brickel, to say a few
words."*

Naomi Brickel, Adam's mom (me):

*"I'm grateful to be here and to those thoughtful enough to
consider this invitation. My hope is to channel a bit of Adam here.
Without question there are messages that have come through strongly*

since his death - mostly from you, in letters and emails from classmates, dreams some were generous to share, stories of his life. Perhaps I could have channeled better lip-syncing Kanye West, but somewhat out of Adam fashion I'm going to be more serious, and bring him here through his 3 big messages:

"Lesson 1: Everything is going to be ok - There's lots on social media about feeling bad for this class of 2020. A class who as sophomores experienced sudden shocking deaths first of Omar and Rolando, then Adam, and then Valerie, and unrest and even violence over that spring. Even if you did not directly know any of them you were impacted and shaken by their loss. This year a football team lost their coach inexplicably in the midst of what was to be THE season. A media spotlight on our community ensued, and enough pressure to crush any realistic dreams. Everyone doubted, and we all felt so bad for you. And Covid! No school, no prom, no graduation, uncertainty about college in the fall.

"Life sure has been tough for the New Ro class of 2020. But I gotta tell you, I don't feel sorry for you at all. It's hard when I'm filled with such pride and inspired by such hope. You learned from the blessings that rose out of those 4 deaths, left to you in the stories of their very different lives and their attributes of authenticity and kindness that don't seem typical in kids so young. You went on. A football team stayed above the drama and with grace and courage brought home a state championship. And for many of you in this class, Covid seems to be nothing more than a somewhat emotional inconvenience. I'm hopeful that into this damaged world a group like you is coming of age. Yes, Adam. It is going to be ok.

"Lesson 2: Don't be fake - I can't tell you how many young men in the class of 2020 wrote to me or shared stories of how Adam had left them with this. Actual real stories and lessons learned, with changes in behavior and how you would treat others after. You are

18

graduating into a world which, especially over the last few months, seems to be lacking authenticity in how the adults in charge are running the show. As our future leaders, you might have the answer in those simple words of Adam's, 'Don't be fake.'

"Lesson 3: The humanity of each person - Finally, Adam had this way of seeing people who others might have missed. It is perhaps what I am most proud of. I recall at a ceremony here that spring for all 4 kids who had died, one young man sharing a story of Adam. They were in the same Chemistry class, and though they didn't really know each other, he spoke of Adam's genuine smile each day for everyone. One day Adam walked in, looked, smiled, and went to his seat across the room. This young man said that the next thing he knew Adam was standing over him saying, "Yo, you don't look so good, are you ok?" He wasn't, and he told him. He said that Adam put his hand on his shoulder (this kid was a year older) and said, "Don't worry, man. Everything is going to be ok. I promise" (reinforcing lesson 1).

That's one of my favorite stories.

"And while people were busy worrying about all of you and how you all were suffering due to quarantine, what did I experience from the class of 2020? I got texts, checking on me to see if I was ok. Thank you Tristan and Ella, Jamie, Corey Baron, Laura Valencia, Nora Fitz, Ava. On random days, out of the blue, thinking of me while everyone was worried about you.

"I'm sad of course that Adam is not here. I will be emotional. Of course, Adam would say that I cried at all the other graduations too, so don't focus on the negative, it's normal.

"It may sound weird, but I don't believe Adam's life was cut short. Many do not know that as a young child I found Adam in his crib one day purple and lifeless. Just about a year old, and nearly gone. We were able to get him back, I suspect because his life still had a

purpose. *Perhaps these messages you've shared with me that I now I relay back are connected.*

"In Adam's loss I am left with a sad and painful hole. But I'm filled simultaneously by the joy of the love I now share with so many of you I did not know before. It is not the same. But it is so rich.

"Maybe in Adam's short life he achieved his purpose. And perhaps these three messages may accompany some of you in the way you shape the world. And perhaps the hole that is left by his physical death becomes filled exponentially with his infinite kind spirit.

"If so, thank you in advance. I love you class of 2020. Congratulations!

Mike

Later the same day via text:

Hey Naomi, today is very great day for our friends they are graduating but I can't get it off my mind that Adam should be there too! I am upset that he isn't there and tomorrow when I graduate (from Iona Prep) I will cry because I know that he is smiling looking down at me proud that I did it and accomplished the goal of graduating! It's hard for me today but I am keeping my head up and cheering for my friends that are graduating! I'm going to visit his tree and send a prayer out to him and hopefully he hears me! I love you Naomi thank you for everything you have done for me and my friends these past few years I don't know where I would be without you and Adam in my life 🖤🖤🖤

I've cried many times with my friends over the past month between prom and thinking about graduation it's hard that he isn't with us 😢

I know it's a rough day for you but I don't
know who to go to in these times where I feel
like a piece of myself is missing! I just wish he
was here

> *Hi mike. Today is a hard day. How*
> *about we go to his tree together?*

Mike is one of Adam's many friends. He's not the only one of his friends (and now mine) who reached out to me on this heart-wrenching day which would have marked such a significant milestone. Many of them texted when they could have simply focused on their own well-deserved happiness, and so did many of their moms and dads. I also received texts and Facebook messages from people I did not even know who had kids that were graduating and had seen the recording of my address to the class. It was moving, and I was fulfilled to be included. And since Mike is the friend who happened to reach out in that specific moment with those specific words; and because he actually attended a different high school and would be graduating the following day, rather than with Adam's New Rochelle High School class, he was the one who came to meet me at "the tree."

Adam's Tree

Adam died around three years ago. He was a sophomore at New Rochelle High School. He would have been in the graduating class of 2020, a class that, in addition to enduring several dramatic episodes during their time in high school, spent the last months of their senior year finishing up credit requirements at home due to Covid. Their high school years were marked by several newsworthy incidents for our New Rochelle community, including being the epicenter of the U.S. Coronavirus outbreak.

New Rochelle High School is a large school in a beautifully diverse city. It is the only public high school for the whole city, and one of the largest in the country, with an annual enrollment of around 3500 students. The demographics are wonderfully reflective of a community that cherishes its cultural variation. The student population is close to 50 percent Hispanic, just under 25 percent each Black and White, with another small percentage consisting of a mix of many other cultures. The school occupies a beautiful and vast, almost castle-like, building sitting behind twin lakes. It is magnificent to look at. People liken it to Hogwarts in the Harry Potter Series.

"Adam's tree" is in front of the left lake. It is accompanied by a small memorial stone that says, "In Loving

Memory, Adam Brickel, 2002 - 2017" and a bench with an inscribed metal plaque that says, "Adam Brickel, Let your Soul Shine" (more on that later). Both were donated by my mom and her bridge group. I love their existence there and go visit often.

After Adam's death I learned a lot about his life in that school, almost all of which was previously unknown to me. I did not really know any of his friends while he was alive, and I had no idea he had so many close friends from numerous diverse groups and backgrounds. I'm blessed that many have become close to me and an integral and important part of my life now. Equally beautiful is their own strong connections, much more than the typical high school cliques and tenuous groupings. They are each individually so important to the whole group. A few of them became couples. I can't help but feel Adam is still there in the midst of it. I know their powerful bond has much to do with him.

In my mourning process, I have been conflicted with how the memories, from those first moments after finding him, the entire crisis on the street, and the whole experience up to confirming his death with the doctor in the ER, evoke little or no emotion for me in recollecting. I've felt frustration and angst and spent time in therapy discussing it. An interesting phenomenon though is how my emotion is provoked, sometimes very intensely, through experiences, either imagined or retold, of initial moments of discovery for others. One of those is Adam's close friend, perhaps one of the closest, Avery.

I never knew or spoke with Avery's mom, Ann, while Adam was alive, except for one phone call the summer before. I was away and realized, shamefully, on a Sunday morning that he had not texted the night before, and I had no idea where he was or if he had made it home safely. I began to panic and imagine the worst. I remembered that Ann had texted one time to confirm the kids plans, and I had saved her number. She was in my contacts as "Ann Avery's Mom." Even as our friendship has now become close, I have kept it that way. I find I do things like that a lot, not wanting to change anything from how it was while he was here. I texted her.

> *Hi. This is Naomi, Adam's mom.*
> *I'm trying to find Adam. Is he*
> *with Avery?*

She responded Immediately. Thank God.

Hi Naomi. I'll call to see if
they're awake. My sitter is over
with the baby so she can check
too. Get right back to you.

He was alive! I didn't even let on how I really truly didn't know where he was. Ann and I reconnected again months later, ironically, just the day before Adam died. Avery was planning to ride with Adam to the NRHS state semifinal football game outside of Albany, NY, and she wanted to get more details about how they were all getting there. It was providential that we had that connection. Avery would stay close in those first months, stopping off to see Jude and JohnPaul often. This enabled Ann and I to become close too, I love her deeply.

She invited me out around a month after. We discovered a mutual affinity for dirty martinis, and laughed and cried a lot. She gave me two bracelets made of stone to promote strength and healing, which I did not take off until Adam's 18th birthday. I think it was that night, there at the bar, where she told me how she and Avery had heard about Adam.

It was the morning after, November 13th, and she was driving him down the hill from her house to the school (they lived right nearby but he was running late). The phone rang.

"Hi Ann. It's Meghan."

I grew up with Meghan, and we knew each other well, coming from large families in the same town and having attended the same catholic schools with friends in common, siblings who are still close, and kids, nieces, and nephews who are all good friends. Her son, Tommy, was also one of Adam's close friends, and her nephew Kevin, one of Johnny's, the first to show up as soon as we arrived from the hospital. Meghan must have heard from her sister, Kevin's mom.

"Hi Meghan. What's up?" Ann answered on speaker.

"Ann, I'm sorry. I'm calling with bad news. Adam Brickel died last night."

"What?!?! Adam?!?! Noooooooo!!!!! Adam!! Noooooooo!!" Avery screamed out and broke down there in the car.

Hearing Ann relay that story, my emotion was triggered about the shock of his death in a way it had not been prior. Even still, recounting this memory is intense, heartbreaking, and emotional. My eyes fill with tears. It is strange how certain people's experiences do that, even as my own arouse nothing.

Avery was the first outside the family, after Kit (my older daughter) and then JohnPaul and I, to memorialize Adam with a tattoo. On Adam's birthday two years later, I got a text from Ann. It was a picture of Avery flexing his muscle with the date of Adam's death in Roman numerals across his bicep.

Yes Avery, he's forever with you now. Forever "Brotha."

And for me, Adam's life is most represented in all of the friends, memories, and stories of his New Rochelle High School experience. So much that we decided to rest his ashes there in front of the tree, Adam's tree. It is, of course, particularly meaningful for me to go there when I want to be close to him; and it was important for me to be there on what would have been his graduation day. I was happy Mike reached out. For me, being with him would bring a little more of Adam to the experience of that important day.

Adam's Day

The high school is about a mile and a half's walk from our house, and when I arrived there were many people around. The distribution of diplomas was still going on, and I could hear the names being announced over the PA system across the lakes. Because this was happening in the middle of Covid, it had been planned differently from previous tradition.

Graduation was always held on the McKenna Football Field, in back of the high school, where families and loved ones watched and cheered from the surrounding stands and bleachers. This year, in order to ensure safety and "social distance," the actual ceremony (including the award and address I had been invited to receive and give) had been pre-recorded days earlier and streamed online that morning. The students went to the high school afterward with their families, got out of their cars to walk across an outdoor stage, receive their diplomas and get a picture, and then returned to their cars and drove away. This year, instead of the stage on the football field, it was situated in one of the large parking lots right behind the lakes. It felt special - and admittedly, deliberately Adam - that because of the changed location, and his resting place by the lake, that in a real sense he was at his graduation. It hit me as I stood there watching.

When I arrived at the bench, many of the students and families were still congregating taking pictures. Several took turns posing on his bench, laughing and celebrating their day around him. I stood back and watched, appreciating his inclusion alongside my sadness over his not being here in person. Adam remains very present, in some ways more than when he was alive, and I felt him. What happened while I was there reinforced it.

I saw Mike walking to meet me while he was still several hundred yards away. It gave me time to watch and appreciate him, and it made me happy. He has a wonderful smile and outlook. He likes to talk about deep things surrounding Adam's life and death, but he is still goofy and funny. It took longer for me to get to know Mike than some of Adam's other friends, but he has become one of the ones I am closest to, and he texts me often. I see and understand how he and Adam would have enjoyed each other; I can almost experience the types of conversations and jokes they would have enjoyed. When he got to me, despite Covid, we hugged, and while he was holding me, unexpectedly, we both wept. I tend not to cry easily in front of people, so it took me by surprise, but I've gotten more comfortable sharing myself and my feelings; and it was good for both of us. We both felt the hole of Adam's absence, and even in our acceptance it was poignant. I'm glad we shared that mutuality; it brought Adam there between us.

We stood awhile and the bench cleared of graduates taking selfies, so we went and sat. Mike was commenting on some of the details he had appreciated in my speech and referred to the part about "being fake." He shared a memory, laughing as he recounted a time when Adam had been stubbornly annoyed with him. The details were reminiscent of a surly side of Adam

I could now vividly recall, and I couldn't help but chuckle. Adam could be a real pain in the ass when he was annoyed or angry. That part of him had faded, and hearing Mike laugh as he said, "He would get so mad sometimes!" brought some of him back, and I laughed too. Yes, he could; I loved being able to re-experience it!

We continued to talk about other things, like Mike's plans for the fall and some of his high school experiences. As he shared, I looked around at the graduates, surveying to see anyone I knew, experiencing a sense of joy and pride in all of these kid's accomplishments.

I noticed a girl and her father among the crowd, walking towards us. The father was wearing a white fedora, and though I could not remember either of their faces as having been among the thousand people at my house over the two days of visitation, their presence permeated me, and I felt quite sure they had. What the man (or the man who I thought he was) had said when he brought his daughter to our house that night had moved me tremendously and left a strong memory, despite so many others. Even if their faces were foggy, the memory and the feelings that seeing the two of them evoked were crystal clear. It felt odd to approach people I didn't know. In a practical sense, it was more likely that these were not the same people, so I stayed put on the bench with Mike. But with each step they took towards and then past us, I was more drawn to them, and as they passed and the distance gained between us, my heart got me up. I interrupted Mike, "Wait, sorry, give me one second" and I ran over to them.

"Excuse me... Hello! Excuse me, were you a friend of Adam's?"

The girl turned back to look at me, checking to be sure my voice was directed at her, "Yes. Hi! Yes, I was!" She smiled and appeared to recognize me.

"I'm Adam's mom. Congratulations. I think I remember you." And then looking at her father, "Did you both come to the house?" And back at the girl, "I'm sorry, I forget your name."

"I'm Tiniya," she replied.

"Yes. We were at your house. I brought Tiniya," her dad responded kindly.

"I thought I remembered you, and I had to come over. It meant so much to me that you came to the house, and the things you said. I remember you thanked me for having people in my house because you felt welcome to come since it was our home. You said beautiful things about how you had to bring Tiniya because Adam had made her so happy; and how she talked about him all the time at home, so much that you felt like you knew him, and how he made her laugh. I have always remembered it. It meant so much to me that you came. Your words that night were a gift I have never forgotten. I'm so happy I saw you and came over!"

We shared some small talk and back and forth, and finally, "Well, I'm so happy I saw you. Is it ok to give you a hug?" I felt a bit awkward, especially in the midst of Covid, but we all embraced anyway. As I hugged Tiniya, I felt Adam in me, as if he himself was here hugging his classmate at their graduation, this friend who loved how he had made her laugh. I felt his joy pouring out into her in our embrace. I was the proxy for their graduation goodbye hug, hugging Tiniya just as Adam would have if he had been there in person. I felt his happiness, and knew he was present, a part of the celebration just like everyone else.

There was not a doubt in my mind that Adam enjoyed his graduation, very much.

Darkness

Back Home

After Adam was pronounced dead at the hospital and we had said our goodbyes, Amy and Kirsty drove us home. It sounds cold, and it did feel like there should be more to it. I don't remember the ride home but can imagine how horrible it must have been for them. I was numb, my brain, or at least the part that handled the emotions, had shut down; I was in shock. I'm sure that at that point it was more real for each of them than it was for me. It felt long, though the ride is less than ten minutes.

As we approached the house, the burden of the first step forward presented itself painfully as I thought of my family - Doug, the kids, my mom, even the dog, Kelly. I could not protect those entrusted to me the way a mother instinctually tries to shield those she loves from pain, suffering, danger, and trauma. Instead, as the messenger of this unreal and unfathomable tragedy, I would impose it.

Doug would receive the news calmly with minimal emotion. It's not that he was unfeeling, he wasn't at all. But even in the declined state of his illness, he wasn't the one to take up space in a room, fill it with too many of his own words or hot air, or draw attention towards himself. He had always been that way, though as a handsome, athletic (he was a high school and college varsity football quarterback), friendly and easy to laugh guy, he could easily have been more attention seeking. He was humble and always directed the attention to me. If there was a story to be told, I got the stage "Nomie, tell them the time ... ." I organized the fun, dictated our plans, maintained the spotlight, directed the firewood to be restocked, etc.

Together, we had created our family of eight. Coming from a big family myself, I wanted one too, and he had few needs or demands as we went along. We had four boys and two girls, with 12 years between the first and last. Our first four kids came right on top of each other. When the fourth, JohnPaul, was born, our oldest, Billy was still only 4. The gap had widened after, with Adam arriving 3½ years after his brother and Jude surprising us - well, shocking me - 4½ years after that. Adam's death would leave a space of 8 years between the now two youngest boys; though JohnPaul would deliberately ensure Jude never felt the "only child" that such a large age gap might have practically imposed.

Billy, the oldest, was 23 years old when Adam died. He had graduated from SUNY Albany eighteen months before and had just moved back into the house that week after a short stint renting a room from a friend. Billy has always been a gentle soul. I have met no one as sensitive and aware of the dignity of all life he encounters - animal, vegetable, or mineral. He has a unique respect, love, and awe for nature and earth's creatures, with a special love for the sea, evidenced by his tremendous knowledge of aquatic science and a "first job" as a volunteer at the Norwalk Aquarium when he was just 16. This position required more than an hour on the train to Connecticut, plus a transfer. Another affinity of Billy's is people, particularly vulnerable people, including those with disabilities. As a brother of a sibling with autism and a teaching assistant for kids in special education, his capacity for connection and ability to de-escalate moments of crisis is noted to be special and unsurpassed. There is something very simple, but uncharacteristically humane, in the way he appreciates people for their individual dignity and light, rather than what they can do for him.

As Amy pulled in, he was there waiting in the driveway with his friend, staring anxiously into the headlights of her SUV. Christian is one of Billy's closest friends who is frequently around and a comfortable part of our family. He had been there earlier that night chuckling with Adam about the argument the two oldest were having over the injustice of who had gotten away with skipping church.

My heart sank deeper as I saw them both waiting there, eager for an update. I was struck, knowing they were clueless of the life altering news they were about to hear.

"How's Adam?" Billy asked expectantly.

I went to hug him, "Oh, I'm so sorry, Billy. He didn't make it. He's gone." I responded quietly, somberly.

He screamed out in anguish and collapsed in tears into the driveway.

Oh, my God. This was just the beginning.

The Longest Night

I went into the house and told them all. Someone had gotten my mom from her house next door. Amy drove her, Doug and Billy to the hospital to say goodbye. While they were gone, my brother Paul and niece, Dana, came. My sister, Mary Gail (Dana's mom), was away with her husband, John, in Germany. They were returning in the morning and would not hear the news until they landed.

We sat in my cold living room, paralyzed, stunned. We were out of firewood so our big fireplace, typically roaring with warmth, was dark and empty. I tried to turn up the heat but the thermostat was broken, and none of the dozens of throw blankets that we had accumulated over the years were anywhere to be found. I looked in every drawer and closet, frustrated and annoyed at Doug, assuming he had stuffed them somewhere in an attempt to clean and now was forgetting. (I would find out later that my blame was misdirected. The culprit had actually been Adam.)

Those who went to the hospital returned. My mom came to embrace me. "Kitty," as she is known by all her grandchildren, and now children too (as well as pretty much anyone who knows her through any of us), lives right next door. She had moved from the big home we grew up in in the next town to a smaller house almost 20 years ago, after my dad had died. And then about a year prior, she had become our neighbor.

Kitty purchased her new home next door from our friends, Ernie and Maggie, whose sons', Ryan and Ethan, were lifelong playmates of Adam, straddling him in age by a year on either side. When they had put their house on the market, to go live in their dream home, Kitty had noticed the sign in the yard. She immediately called my sister, who was also a realtor.

"Mary Gail, the house next door to Naomi is on the market. I want that house. We need to put in an offer. Whatever it takes."

"Mom, you can't put in an offer on a house you haven't even seen." She had responded reasonably.

"I have seen it! You used to live there!" Coincidentally, my only sister's first home was actually the house next door, though she had moved from it over 25 years before, long before Doug and I purchased ours. It was (and still is) now my mom's, enabling our daily visits, regular glasses of wine, relationships with my kids, and a short walk after being woken by Billy and Kit with the tragic news.

Kitty was grave. As I looked at her pained face I knew that she understood too well what I was to endure. I am the fifth child in a family of seven kids, and ten years earlier she had lost her son, my oldest brother, Brian. As she came to me, I was still in shock, but of course she wasn't. Intellectually, I realized how painful it had to be to watch a child experience such a tragedy, one of which she had firsthand knowledge. I recall thinking that perhaps the only thing worse than losing a child is watching your own child go through such a loss and being powerless to protect her.

Brian, the second oldest, eight years my senior, had also died suddenly of a cardiac issue at 46 years old, an aortic aneurysm. We discovered Adam's condition (as well as my own and JohnPaul's) when we were all tested after he died. Ironically, Adam and I had been diagnosed with two conditions associated with sudden death during that testing years earlier. We both had HCM and the condition that had caused my brother's death, a dilation, and for Brian subsequent dissection, of the aorta.

It would be months before I would have Adam's final autopsy report (I still had doubts about the ER doctor's conclusion) confirming that he had died of an arrhythmia associated with his HCM. And during that long wait I would be reminded of it daily since the county medical examiner's office was right behind my office.

I returned to work after two weeks; it was too soon. I felt pressured by no one but myself, the only one who could not see the tragedy objectively. Each day as I walked through the front doors into the lobby, I saw the building in the distance. Imagine walking into work every day and looking out at the building where your son's body is being autopsied, where lab specimens with his flesh lie waiting for results, for 20 weeks. What a sick painful irony. Even today that building is the harsh landmark I notice when I walk through the doors at the beginning of my work day. Work from home has been a Covid silver lining in that regard.

My mom was 83 the night Adam died, a strong happy and young 83. But even so, I was frightened by how this horrible trauma might impact her. I became serious in my response to her embrace. "Mom, you have to be strong and careful. I need you to take care of yourself. Don't try and do everything and overdo it. I am going to need you after this and can't afford to lose you anytime soon." My mom is a best friend, and we are an active part of each other's lives; I knew could not lose her on top of everything else.

It was 1:00 or 2:00 a.m. when we were all home beginning our new life together without him. The minutes passed slowly with nothing to do but sit. It was too late to notify or connect with people, but how could anyone go to bed? The hours ahead were daunting, like an imminent journey through the desert, and yet each minute that passed was its own threat, taking me further from his life, from him. I was desperate for time to stop, even as the impending hours felt interminable, and found myself fighting and wishing their passing. All of this was compounded by a menacing knowledge that tomorrow evening, eventually, and every night after, I'd have to go to bed, confronting the reality of my precious child's death, of Adam's loss, in the dark, alone.

And so progressed the longest night of my life.

Alone

This morning I woke up alone,
like any other
the alarm, darkness,
a push forward, typical effort from rest,
Reluctant yet resigned.

Today Alone had an escort,
came attended,
by Loneliness,
the unfortunate companion
of an otherwise benign state.

Achingly arduous
supressingly crushing
depressed, deflated
extinguished, enervated
feeble and fatigued,

I rise out of bed
like every other morning,
But the effort drains me,
the impending day,

Not the 'alone' - I have the strength for solo
But Loneliness...

The weight of concern

Kids-
their pain, direction, steps not taken, missteps
appointments to be made

Work -
loose ends, long days, sole responsibility, complex people

Finances -
ends not met, bills outstanding, insurance refusals

The Future -
the perpetual abyss of my losses,
empty space where I long to lean...
even the therapist is gone.

What makes today different?
Not the details or burdens,
Or the support or love free to me,

Hope is half-hearted.

Death's Darkness

About a year after he died, I read a book about the untimely, sudden death of a child. I have never cracked the spines of most of the other books that were given to me after Adam died, except one other. All were given in kindness, by people I love deeply and respect, offered in hope they would bring comfort, perspective, or possibly the tools needed to get through such a horrific tragedy - every parent's worst nightmare. Though I enjoy self-help literature, I have not had any desire to read anything about this: to learn lessons about hope, or how to cope, or do my son's death the best way. For the most part I've been content in my own process (and at times not content with anything). In those first days and months I survived one minute at a time, slowly progressing to an hour, then several, and even to days by around a year and a half. Even now, as I have become more filled with peace (after much work and therapy), I deliberately work on my willingness to be in and out of sadness and accepting that the darkness is an appropriate place to be, and always does (hopefully) open to light.

I read this book because of who gave it to me, my neighbor Amy, with whom I have experienced a lot over our lifetime, including growing up in the same neighborhood, elementary and high schools, new houses side by side, simultaneous pregnancies, kids becoming best friends and like siblings to one another, joyful, scary, and sad moments, reoccurring flour, eggs, mustard, and other daily necessities neighbors share when one is lacking, family dinners, glasses of wine … and Adam's death. The same Amy who was with me that night, from the initial moments of discovery until my ultimate leaving him forever as she drove me in her car from the hospital. I've always loved her as my neighbor, but of course there is something deeper and more unbreakable now.

So, I read this book that she and her daughter, Caroline, brought home from a trip to Lebanon. The book is called *Crossing*. It is written by Zeina Kassem, a mother who also lost her son, Talal, unexpectedly and tragically, like me, like Adam.

While I could never diminish the process of any mother who has endured the loss of a child, some of her experience did not connect for me when I first started reading. Maybe it was too soon; I wasn't interested in another's experience presented as an example of how to do it right. It's not as if I perceived myself as either more or less courageous, feeling, or better or worse in any way. There is no right way to do the loss of your son, or any other type of grief for that matter. Whatever way one gets through it is good, and whatever feels right probably is. It was okay that I wasn't connected to this mom's experience. We shared everything important in common in the sudden devastating losses of our beautiful and magnetic teenage sons. I've never met her, but she's in my heart with my immense admiration and pride, like a sister, as our experience bonds any who have lived it. I ached for what she endured, and was proud of her courage and strength to share her voice.

Yet there was something that did resonate: Chapter 8. Here Zeina described the unalterable permanence of the injury of losing a child. And the way she articulated it shattered any protective compartmentalization I had achieved for my own pain. As I read her description of her new reality my chest tightened and I began to feel hopeless, afflicted, and threatened by a sudden cognizance that I'd repressed - this would always be part of me: I may be strong and resilient on the outside, and in fact I am; I may be happy in a moment, and I truly am; but always, under any healing or happiness, my primal reality lurks... Adam's death. It scared the sh-- out of me. I was nauseous.

Nothing is like the loss of a mother's child. I say that with the credibility of experience having lost two close friends in my youth, a sibling, a parent, and currently living in the throes of losing my husband of almost 30 years, who is in the late stages of a terminal illness that has stolen his body and mind (I'm only in my early 50's). All of these experiences were difficult, but losing my son is an entirely different loss.

It's true, that especially during the first two years after Adam's death, everything else, my day to day life, and even my grief and healing process, were just peripheral details. His loss was my only relevant reality, and it was pervasive. I remember during the first weeks, one of the first days I was back in my office, sitting at my computer and thinking, "How does any of this ever matter again?" Stephanie, a mom of four, sat closest to me at the time. In that moment she must have read my mind and asked, "Do you ever think about anything else but him? Does it ever leave your mind?"

"No, it really doesn't, but somehow I can still do stuff." So much of my life was just happening by default, going through motions, cruise control.

Such a loss is isolating - from everyone - even those you most love and cherish. I was in a cold, dark, engulfing cave, immersed deeply in a cloudy grey existence. In moments of love or joy I still experienced solitude. In the midst of friends or family, engaged and perhaps even laughing, I remained disconnected (even today, I still talk less). My cave was for one, and I was deeply lonely in the remoteness, feeling separated even in a crowd. But I had no desire to come out or be included.

There was a particular instance about a year after. I was preparing for Christmas, surprised how well my grief was contained at the holidays. I was alone fixing the tree, arranging the lights so that the kids at home would be able to decorate together later. This was how we had always done it. They were much older now, didn't care the same way, and certainly would not fight about who got to hang the angel ornament (as Adam and Mindy always had), but it was still how it had to be done. Traditions are even more important now, especially ones he was part of.

I was on the floor underneath the tree reaching for the outlet to plug in the lights. Stomach to floor, flat under the lowest branches, I extended my body and arms reaching to plug it in. As I stretched, my head naturally rose up, and the shelf hidden behind the tree came into sight. There he was, Adam, a black box of ashes. No one even knew he was there all this time, on a shelf, while we waited for him to somehow communicate a final resting place. The severity of the cold plastic container, his container, hit me and my grief broke open, there on the floor under the tree, such an odd precarious position. If I moved the wrong way or too much in any direction, I'd knock the whole thing over, but I desperately needed to be there. Pathetically, I maneuvered into the deep corner, up under and behind the tree, and negotiated the box off the shelf. Here he was at Christmas, alone and ignored. I took the sterile box with the lifeless remains of his once virile body, holding him in my lap for longer than my life generally allows. I sat crying, coddling, holding, comforting, never wanting to leave him or be okay. Could we just remain there together always? Calculatingly, I positioned myself so if someone walked in (my house is like a bus station), it would not look so strange and pitiful. They could assume I was fixing lights, arranging the electrical cords, whatever. I just never wanted to leave.

And a half hour later I was back in my kitchen: cooking, cleaning, organizing, visiting, smiling, and showing all that life is okay. Back in the routine, minutes after the immense trauma of holding my dead son at Christmas. It must sound despairing and hopeless; it's certainly been devastating and dark.

As a child is generated from his mother's body, they share actual physical being. It is a different type of love and connection than any other. His flesh develops from hers and the two are physically connected for both of their lives. The scar is permanent when the child dies first. An actual tangible part of the mother herself is gone, perhaps like losing a limb. Because of this connection, a mom feels the experiences of her child as if they were her own. When her child is in pain, the mother experiences pain. Perhaps more deeply even. When the child excels, her pride in him is exponentially her own pride. When her child is sick, the mother is sick inside. When a child is born with a disability (I speak from personal experience), a mother can be so overcome with grief and the instinctual need to protect and fix that her own reactive behaviors become disabling. Moms have a hard time not spoiling their children. It requires her own self-discipline to let the child experience hard lessons. Being firm is like being hard on oneself; giving in, or making something easier on them, an indulgence ... Perhaps God created dads to whip them into shape!

Lovers or spouses can share deep genuine love, soulmates so deeply and intimately connected, so close, that they get into each other's heads and read each other's minds. However, other than those rare moments of incredible intimacy, they are still separate. They can have competing interests and get on each other's nerves. A lover or spouse, even in the deepest loving relationship, can still be selfish or self-serving and capable of compromising the needs of the other for their own. A mother can't. Although there are always exceptions, a mother, usually from the moment of joyful discovery of his conception, gives over her interests and identity to her child. When my oldest was born I transformed from "Naomi" to "Billy's Mom," As my youngest, Jude, 14, transitions to adulthood 26 years later, I'm just beginning to feel my individual identity resurface, and I don't necessarily welcome it. Even this normal developmental separation is accompanied by its own grief. It took a whole recent session in therapy. It's hard to let go of your offspring.

It makes sense then that the death of a child comes with such incomparable, unalterable and horrible permanence. A person in remission from cancer lives with the awareness that it is always a part of them, either in the repercussions of the toxic treatment that may last a lifetime, or the knowledge that at any moment it could resurface. They may forget if the after-effects are minimal or things are good for a long time and the risk appears to have dissipated, but it's still there. Adam's loss, too, is ever present. It has gradually become bearable - but never absented (if that makes any sense). And I actually don't ever want it to because that would somehow imply further separation.

His death became my most real reality.

Flashlights

Kind Wisdom

When I was young
inspired by Solomon
I prayed for Wisdom
and his generous intent.

To nurture Wisdom
He let me suffer.
I learned to accept
become dependent,
When I had nothing
I endured in Him.

To inspire Generosity
He gave me children.
I learned to sacrifice
and give everything,
Once I was empty
He had room to dwell.

Now I'm older
Am I wiser, more kind?
Or just tired and humbled
And resting in His love?

Liberated in dependence

Adam's Purpose?

The just man, though he die early, shall be at rest.
For the age that is honorable comes not with the
passing of time, nor can it be measured in terms of
years ... He who pleased God was loved; he who
lived among sinners was transported ... Having
become perfect in a short while, he reached the
fullness of a long career; for his soul was pleasing
to the LORD ... . But the people saw and did not
understand, nor did they take this into account.
Because grace and mercy are with his holy ones,
and his care is with the elect.

The Book of Wisdom 4:7-15

So, how does a mom get from the devastating tragedy of November 12, 2017 to a happy sunny day 2½ years later for her dead son's high school graduation, hopeful sentiments in a speech and joyful hugs, much less write a book relating to such dark circumstances with a happy ending right in the title?

When I started writing, I did not set out to write a memoir of me or my dead son or any lessons learned in processing his death. The insights of people more brilliant than I fill that shelf already. There are countless narratives written by famous and well-established people with platforms, people who are culturally relevant, important, and wise. There's hardly room for another, much less from an unknown me. I grew up in a family of seven kids, on the young side of the middle of five brothers. My early life experiences were closer to "The Lord of the Flies" than a breeding ground for self-importance. I'm not so brazen as to put myself out there as wise or important, nor would Adam want that, or for his life to be attached to a book about death. He was a prankster and clown, in mostly self-deprecating ways, and would never have projected himself with any solemnity or importance.

I just got an urge to write. It was a persistent need to get things down "on paper," all of it, the darkest moments and the blessings that came after. I didn't know what I was trying to accomplish. Perhaps I was desperate to maintain his memory, to ensure that, even in his death, he was not completely obliterated by the passing of time. Truth be told, it has been an ongoing threat how his life and earthly existence, decisively ended by his sudden death, continue to move further from the present.

There were also wonderful stories, signs, blessings - so many lights - that I did not want to lose or forget. They had come unexpectedly from the first moments, in the stories kids told when they visited the house, dreams people shared, my own experiences, and little strange occurrences eerily resonating his trademark unorthodox ways. Adam clearly impacted so many during his life here on earth and left a wake, a beautiful inclusive wave that encompassed and moved so many. So, I decided to try and get it all down in one place, if only for myself. But I began to wonder as I went if the process of writing might help me tease out a message.

Months later, with most of it written, I know Adam has been here enlightening the whole time. He gradually presented a purpose, not about death, but about living, and as simplistic as it sounds (and so Adam), about seeing light and being "happy" - so relevant to the time and circumstances. As I recalled and relived separate, wonderful stories, I started to notice themes with surprising relevance for my life in all of its chaos, bumps and hardships, and for our world right now.

As I continue to navigate this perpetual (but less prevalent) ache almost three years later, I'm keenly aware of the lights along the way, accompanied by the grace to notice them, providing the perseverance to live. There was something very real - perhaps Hope - that pierced the gloom in certain moments, where something made me stop and notice. From the very beginning my grey damp cave, despite its ever-present reality and cold darkness, displayed lights. Minute by minute, day by day, noticing them facilitated my survival. Like water breaks along a marathon route, they didn't necessarily make it easier, but offered respites and distractions from the otherwise incessant tribulation. Without these interspersed recharging sparks, and the actual connection with them, the experience would have been an otherwise constant and pervasive despairing dark torment.

Almost as if I had fallen so far down into a deep well where light couldn't at first penetrate (the despondency associated with losing a child is that thick), my sight needed to adjust. I gradually began to access capacities I had not used previously, new faculties enabling me to perceive life in ways I never had, drawn from something deep inside, but at the same time more powerful than I. From the very first hours I noticed things, quickly obfuscated by the immense consuming grief. It was a process, a long road filled with grief, anger, pain, sweat, tears, and time, to get acclimated to, notice, or even be willing to acknowledge lights, but I would only be sharing half of it if I didn't. Today, they are still as real and present, and even light up my cave brightly - acknowledging its enduring presence.

My personal challenge through this has been to develop an acceptance, understanding, and certainty about suffering - my children's suffering, the sadness of my family and close friends, and his most dear friends, even Adam's death itself - similar to how one experiences the changing seasons.

As I poured myself into writing during most of July 2020, embraced in warmth, love and laughter of family and friends, the beach, festive outdoor dinners of summer's bounty, under twinkling lights hoisted in a magnificent lush tree, I could reflect on and easily accept the realization that December in all of its dark, cold, barrenness, and bone chilling pain had gotten me there, from the subtle moment that the short dark days began to get longer just before Christmas. Most important, is the simple, obvious, but relevant fact, I lived through it. As I shivered, woke up in the dark, hid my face from icy rain pulling garbage to the curb, or shoveled the snowy walk, I never questioned the laws of nature, but was steadfast in hope and certainty of the coming warm and bright summer days. March Covid shutdowns opened to summer outdoor dining in the streets, walks on the beach, socially distanced backyard visits, and dinners with friends and family. And I made it!

As I wrote and reflected in July's vibrant light, I was able to perceive Adam's death and all of the pain and associated suffering metaphorically, and gain a certain awareness that out of the tragedy of my beloved's death, there was also something new and beautiful. I was able to tap a fountain of knowledge deep within me, right beneath the base of my lowest rock-bottom: a Wisdom that, as Adam would have said when he was alive, "It's all Good."

Examples of this are evident in my expanded capacity for hope and in how I now see people and situations in new ways, looking past distracting or complicating traits to the human person inside. In much the same way that I found my own treasure, my own light, buried underneath the darkest depths of an otherwise distracting and consuming anguish, I have grown in my tendency to see beyond the complexities of others, past what might sometimes manifest as annoying, unattractive, even seemingly hopeless, to a person's individual internal light. I am able to recognize and appreciate graces I took for granted before, like the joy of my kids' existence, presence, and personalities, rather than be consumed with angst or worry over their paths or problems. I have become true to what is important in myself without concern for what others think. I can curl up in tears and despair under my Christmas tree at one moment, but hours later feel joy in my blessings as I laugh with the kids over the fact that Mindy had no competition for the angel ornament (Adam always beat her to it). I am more adept at seeing light and blessings, even when I'm resigned to the cave in the depths of sorrow, and I don't need to fight or resist my sadness or make it better. Instead, I can acknowledge that a mother who loses her child was designed by nature, or God (whichever your preference, to me they are interchangeable), to be sad, but that it doesn't mean life isn't still precious or hasn't happened as it was meant to.

I believe that from the beginning Adam was with me encouraging my awareness. If I only noticed or spoke about the sadness and despair it would be half the story - like biased news with facts omitted in order to add drama, but presenting a "fake" truth and tainted reality. There isn't a doubt in my mind now that Adam was alongside all of us through these last years, perhaps (hopefully) here still, directing and facilitating a message. For a mom, shrouded in grief, fully distracted in my misery, and utterly consumed with trying to keep life going, he needed to be perseverant and make his communication obvious. My gift was noticing, rather than remaining blinded by the sadness or lost in my despair.

I'm amazed by how "big ideas" broke through in the course of my writing, after the patient planting of seeds from the first hours after his death (the stories I was writing about). One instance of this was critical. I was writing about a book, *Embraced by the Light* by Betty Eadie, given to me by Ms. Stella, a middle school teacher who taught most of my kids, including Adam. We had reconnected at Jude's "meet the teacher" night, a few months after she had lost her partner, and she suggested we get together. We enjoyed a wonderful happy hour sharing details of our horrible life tragedies. After, she sent me the book with a note saying she hoped it would bring me some comfort as it had for her. It did. This book became a major milestone in my healing and I ordered 25 copies and gave it out at Christmas.

When she first gave it to me, though, I wasn't sure I was up for it and put it in my bag. I was on the train riding back from the city a week or so later and noticed everyone staring down at their phones. Inspired to engage my brain more productively, I took out the book. A best seller from the 90's, it's about a woman's near-death experience, detailing her visions and perceptions of the afterlife. Early on, she shares a memory of a separate near-death experience from her childhood, which includes a loving, tender, heavenly father holding and comforting her as she lies dying from a terrible illness in an orphanage. As I read her recollection, I was suddenly struck by the fact that Adam too had nearly died when he was just a toddler.

The memories of that day 16 years before flooded back to me on the train. Coming home from an afternoon of errands and being told he was still in his crib napping ... feeling annoyed as I went up to wake him knowing he wouldn't sleep that night ... reconsidering as I went to open the door, thinking that as long as he was quiet, I could get organized downstairs first ... turning to go back down ... halfway down reconsidering ... missing him and thinking he shouldn't be alone that long ... turning and running back up ... opening the door, going to his crib, looking down at his head hidden by the tightly wrapped blanket ... "Oh my God!"... frantically untangling ... Adam's purple face and rolled back open eyes ... screaming again ... grabbing and still untangling ... rushing to the car yelling for Doug to grab the keys ... angst, panic, and fear of the unthinkable as I held him in the back seat on the way to the hospital... storming through the ER doors (those same doors and ER where 14 years later he would be pronounced dead), "Help me! Help me! My baby's not breathing!"

Sitting there on the train, my eyes filled with tears as the details of this woman's account connected to Adam. I considered for the first time that perhaps he, too, had an experience during that first crisis. I had never fathomed it - a toddler's near-death experience? He was so little. I always assumed too small to remember. Was it possible that Adam had felt loving arms or even wished he could remain there? Did he share a similar story?

This was what I had chosen to write about one summer day because I thought of it so often. What stayed with me was that the morning after that horrible night so many years ago, he had refused to nap and screamed in his crib, crying inconsolably for hours. I had gone in to soothe him knowing he needed sleep, but refused to give him back the strangling "death" blanket. It was such a painful ordeal hearing him screaming that my friend,

Emily Sullivan, had salvaged it from the garbage and sewn what became his precious "BooBoo Bear" (seeing his attachment, she had made two in case he lost one). But even with his security blanket back, and after being the most endearing, pleasant and loving infant, Adam became a horrible toddler. He developed a permanent bruise from banging his head in temper tantrums, and a raspy voice, his "whiskey- drinking- strained- vocal- cord- lounge- singer's voice." (Formally diagnosed as attributable to excessive screaming, by a real doctor, I had actually been advised to try harder to keep him happy in order to prevent permanent vocal cord damage.) I used to say, and perhaps it's still true, that nobody ever loved or hated me more than "Terrible Two's Adam."

Could it all be connected? Had he experienced something in those brink of death moments as a toddler? Had he come back against his will, or just struggled to transition back to this life after experiencing the beauty of the next? Occasionally he had asked very deep questions about life and death, about his own life and his own possible death. There had been one instance where he had come right out and asked me, "Mom, am I gonna die from my heart thing?" I had reassured him that when families knew about his condition, kids didn't die; we could be proactive, stop playing sports, go to the doctor and get tested each year, just like we did. That would keep him safe, I'd told him. Another time he had reacted strangely when I tried to engage him about his dad's illness. He had gotten very emotional, cried and screamed in a way that was unlike him, but deflecting the issue from himself and expressing angst over his brothers, the potential repercussions of their pain, in a way that was puzzling and strange at the time.

Did he know something? Even subconsciously? I had never contemplated that he even remembered it. I like to think he would have said something at some point if he did. But could it have remained there under his conscious recollection somehow? Was it possible Adam had engaged in some sort of Divine negotiations, that in his willingness to come back, for whatever reason, whatever purpose, he brokered a shorter stay? I've never understood what made me turn around mid-stairwell and go back up to him that day. If I hadn't, he would have been lost as an infant. Was there something to that? A reason? A purpose?

In this lifetime, of course, I'll never have those answers. But something powerful occurred that summer day as I wrote, something important, that changed my perspective completely, forever. Suddenly, I was inspired by the idea that perhaps Adam's life was not cut short at all.

Instead, maybe all those years before it had actually been extended, and a child about to be taken was given more time. Maybe friends he'd not yet met would have access to rich blessings of his kindness, love, and laughter. Perhaps a little brother would come to be born and have the much-needed experience of getting punched around, teased and loved, rather than maybe never being born at all or learning of the phantom older brother through his mother's brokenness, pictures of the child who had died, sad stories, or some sort of shrine. Maybe siblings would have the opportunity to develop meaningful relationships, memories, and love, instead of merely holding onto faint faded images of the baby that died. Perhaps his parents, instead of a marriage broken in despair, might be given 14 precious years to grow and mature from the experiences of knowing and raising him, build memories, make prank phone calls, love and be loved deeply and differently...

And, maybe a sad boy in Chemistry class, rather than suffering alone in silence, would become the subject of a graduation speech, having been moved, comforted, reassured, and yes, loved, by an underclassman he barely knew, provided with the needed encouragement and the important message, "It's gonna be ok."

The curse of a life stolen young was suddenly transformed, in the instant spark of one thought, into the blessing of the gift of life.

The reading from Wisdom at the beginning of this chapter was read at his funeral. Three years later, as I write and recollect, I'm further inspired, able to detect the relationship between a scripture chosen days after his death and this recent "gift of life" epiphany. It's almost like looking from above. It was there all along, of course. My awareness just needed time to gain the acumen of the connection. There is a warm comfort in the "something bigger"-ness of that.

In the pages and recounted experiences that follow, I will try to put words around more of it, to pull together and tie up some loose ends, and perhaps bring more light to his purpose. Knowing so much more about Adam's life now, I feel confident in my perspective (even if he himself was only subconsciously aware during his life). My goal is to stimulate greater awareness, and continue to reinforce my own, in the benevolence and beauty of life, even with all of its suffering. I hope to inspire others, especially today's young people, to not be hopeless or defeated, realizing that big smiles, simple acts of kindness, hope, and authenticity are actually far more powerful than bullying, mean girls, fake news or politicians, anxiety about the future, human violence, or even Covid.

In Adam's memory, and under what I believe is his inspiration in the messages he left and communicated after, I will try (through a 50+ year-old lens) to bring light to the lights, to the simple patterns and Loving energy filling this life and universe - even as it all applies to a mom's worst nightmare - the death of her precious child.

I have grown a lot from his death and my grief, and began to feel empowered from the first hours after his death. I am stronger knowing that what I have experienced is the worst suffering, but I am okay, even better for it. I experience a joy and contentment in life that I did not have the capacity for before, and I know this is exactly what Adam would have wanted.

My biggest lesson so far is that the path to the brightest light, biggest joy, and at least my own overall contentment, was necessarily through the darkest valley and deepest sadness; and it has been worth the journey. As I look back on other periods of suffering, I can see that it is the dark times, and what they demanded in order to cope and get through, that facilitated my blossoming and best growth. Looking back, I would not change my loneliness or rock bottoms, the graces that accompanied me through them, or the subsequent blessings. They shaped me into the person I am satisfied and gratified to be today, still connected but accepting of my sadness over his loss, and also very happy. Living through it has only reinforced and solidified my belief that life is beautiful, happens as it is meant to, and that even the darkest moments come with a flashlight. In hindsight, quite frankly, it seems good and there is not really anything I would change.

Not even his death.

Fruits

But the fruit of the Spirit is love, joy, peace,
patience, kindness, goodness, faithfulness,
gentleness, and self-control. Against such
things there is no law.

St. Paul, *Letter to the Galatians 5:22-23*

  I like to read, though for two years after I did not read anything. Even prior to his death, reading had gotten sidelined by the competing priorities and general stress of my life. About a year before he died, I discovered that there was an audible account in my name. Johnny had set it up in high school so he could listen to rather than read, a school assignment. I realized I had spent $15/month for three years for one dumb, unfinished book. I tried to close it but was convinced by pop-ups begging me to stay and maintain the account for a one-time $9 charge until I used up the remaining credits. One accumulates lots of credits paying for accounts they don't use; so on my commutes to work I began to dive into spiritual awakening and self-help, eating up unused Audible book credits like Pac-man.

  Years prior, I had discovered Fr. Richard Rohr and returned to his works and others. Rohr is a Franciscan Friar well known for his writing on faith and Christian mysticism. His insights have been influential in redirecting my practical spirituality into a greater alignment with my personal faith. There are things about my Catholic religion with which, like many, I struggle, and stuff I just don't get. The focus on rules for who can participate feels exclusionary rather than loving, and the import given to canon directives and prohibitions seems closer to the behaviors of the Pharisees, with whom Jesus was always exasperated, than a church formed out of His inclusive Gospels.

A continuum of sin, from venial (not really too bad) to mortal (straight to Hell) developed by "Church Fathers" over the centuries feels contradictory to the merciful "Abba" (translated Daddy!) to whom Jesus directed us to pray. I question why my childhood was plagued by fears of dying and the threats of Hell when I was raised in a faith based on scriptures in which the most frequent command is "Don't be afraid." Why is our church so scary? Jesus was pretty outgoing, even accepting of sinners and outsiders, and genuine. Fr. Rohr's Franciscan spirituality reawakened my beliefs in a loving rather than calculating and threatening God, reinforcing my inner instincts and that the true faith and message of Jesus was not one of rules and prescriptions, despite how my religion has evolved.

It was Richard Rohr's writings that made St. Paul's words about the spiritual "fruits" in his Letter to the Galatians strike me. I typed it out and printed it, and it hangs over my desk at work. For about a year prior to Adam's death it was there, and until Coronavirus relegated us to home offices, I saw it daily. Every day I would read and reflect on it when I arrived at my desk. I hung it there because when I came across it one particular day, though not for the first time, it resonated as reassuring, reinforcing, and beautiful.

Faith has always been important to me. I attend mass on Sunday and sometimes during the week. I am active in my parish life. My priests are good friends and come over regularly. I was brought up on and still pray the Rosary; I know all of the "holy days of obligation" and other pertinent details of my religion; I do things for Lent. I'm in. But as my faith has matured, I've questioned and challenged the perceived inconsistencies. At times it's unsettling; I second guess, or others question my loyalty. I happen to be imperfect, "a sinner" as the Church puts it - a contingency of membership in this club called "human." I have sometimes felt the insecurity that I wasn't working hard enough, getting it right, perfect. It nagged me, until that day when St. Paul's quote sunk in. I suddenly got the real message: What's important is not the rules or law, but being open, filled and driven by the Spirit, a "Temple of the Divine." I began to strive for that.

I started meditation, admittedly a bit sloppy and slow, about 18 months before Adam died. Every morning on my way into work I stopped at a parish church five minutes from my office, and sat quietly for 20 minutes, monitored by Siri. I would try to quiet my brain, let down my guard, and experience God's presence within me. I incorporated St. Paul's quote in my meditation. With each breath, sometimes several, I would focus on letting each "fruit" emanate my whole being. Breathe in "Love", slowly. Breathe in "Joy," many breaths (since who doesn't want to be happier?), "Peace," exhale, "Patience" ... Take it all in with each breath.

I tried to make room for the Spirit to find space, letting selfish ego-driven thoughts go in my exhales. I envisioned a Divine Presence within my soul, surrounded by a brick wall that was crumbling, letting the Light out into the rest of my person, a union of Spirit and body, emanating out through my smile or interactions with others. When I arrived at my office, seeing the quote over my desk, before settling into work and the day's emails, I'd reflect on a characteristic of a spiritual fruit where I might have fallen short and relive the routines in my mind with more of it in me.

At 4:20am on November 13, 2017, a few stunned hours into my new life and reality as "dead Adam's mom," I got up from our living room couch for a change of scenery. Walking into the kitchen and looking up at the clock, I thought about work. I loved my job and the people I worked with. I work for a nonprofit organization. At that time, overseeing programs assisting in the navigation of disability systems across the lifespan and working with professionals in those systems to develop innovative programs to serve impacted individuals. I had the opportunity to travel and present at conferences, work with wonderful passionate people in my office and across the state and country, and affect policy in the education and adult service systems. Today I'm still in the same organization, engaged in the same work, though it's evolved into a more executive level role with greater involvement in public policy. So many colleagues from everywhere would show up over the next few days and become such a great support over the months and years that followed.

I thought about tomorrow and how my team might react when they heard the news. I wondered whether I would ever have the strength, capacity, passion, will, or ability to focus or work again after going through this night, these next days, weeks, and beyond processing his death. What would I be like? How long would it be until I went back, sat at my desk again, or went through my daily routines? And with that last thought, my morning ritual and the quote from St. Paul came to mind. I sat and recited it silently to myself.

As I went through each "fruit," I envisioned it in Adam. I did not make an effort, the images just emerged - each one so obvious, clear, precise, and exquisite. I saw him Loving. I experienced his Joy in a vibrant smile. I felt the Peace in his calm. On and on... images of his Gentleness with little ones on the trampoline, Self-control one night in a moment of stress in our dining room...

In those numbing first hours, I was filled with a vision of his Immortal Spirit ... somehow it penetrated, and actually brought me Joy.

WholeHeartedness

The Wholehearted journey is not the path of least resistance. It's a path of consciousness and choice. And, to be honest, it's a little counterculture. The willingness to tell our stories, feel the pain of others, and stay genuinely connected in this disconnected world is not something we can do halfheartedly.

Dr. Brené Brown

Months before Adam died I discovered Brené Brown. Those audible credits certainly turned out to be worth it! I was fortunate to have four of her books under my belt at the time of his death and worked on incorporating her findings on authenticity, vulnerability, and wholeheartedness into how I lived. Her ideas fortified aspects of my personality that in my "Irishness" I was inclined to repress. Ideas around "belonging", rather than "fitting in" reinforced my deep, interesting, lifelong friendships. And the idea that it was more important to be in a room where I could be my authentic self than be in the "right" crowd resonated. I have always appreciated the peripheries over inner circles. A close friend once affectionately teased that all my friends are priests or gay. And what's wrong with that? They all showed up for me!

Brown's research around vulnerability resonated. I wear my heart on my sleeve and tend to share and reveal more than others (hopefully not in a screaming way - but hence this book!) At times I've felt exposed or too "soft," yet when I repress "me" it hurts, almost as if I'm hiding, cheating, or a fake. Thanks to Brené Brown, I don't worry about it anymore, and develop more fulfilling connections by sharing my authentic self.

Through her research, she's identified outliers, people who experience greater fulfillment through love and belonging, and by "living and loving with their *whole hearts* (my emphasis) despite the risks and uncertainty." She has detailed traits, "guideposts," that are cultivated among "wholehearted" people, like authenticity, relaxation, faith, resilience, self-compassion, gratitude, and even laughter.

Adam certainly lived with his "whole heart" - ironic considering the cause of death ...

In his homily at the funeral, my pastor, Fr. Thomas, captured Adam's "wholeheartedness." He spoke about how his heart, the organ that pumps blood, was weak and gave out; it literally broke, but that Adam's heart, as the symbolic center of the spiritual inner self, was not broken at all, nor had he died of a broken heart. "A person who dies of a broken heart suffers from love that failed, or a lack of love." Not Adam, a 15-year-old boy who was filled with love and loved, a young man who received and gave so much! He compared Adam's heart to the heart of Jesus, whose physical heart had also stopped at that moment he died on the cross, and how Christ's Heart, during the whole of Jesus' earthly life, was the center from which was manifested, in a human way, the love of God.

I was hungry – you gave me food

I was thirsty – you gave me drink

A stranger – you welcomed me

Naked – you clothed me
Ill – you cared for me
In prison - you visited me

He pointed to Jesus' presence in the needy, how what we do to them, we do to God. At a young age Adam was already living this Gospel, a disciple, but in his own 15-year-old way. Though Adam was a normal kid, one who loved his fancy sneakers (much of Adam's prioritized efforts over the two years before he died surrounded the acquisition of models in the "Yeezy Collection," a line of expensive Adidas sneakers developed by designer, rapper, and entrepreneur Kanye West), there was also something clearly unique, special, and different. "A *normal* teenager, but not an *ordinary* teenager." A heart pumping Love! He referred to things written in the visitation book we had put out at the at the house for kids to share memories and the comments he overheard at the house: "He was kind to me" "He paid attention to me." "He talked to me." "He smiled at me." "He listened to me." "He laughed with me." Not with a select few, not only with those who looked like him, or sounded like him, or came from families like his. He read a text he had received from a parishioner upon hearing the news: "Adam was an old soul with a shining light so bright so special - there are no words to describe it. Adam was a true shining light of God. He radiated love and kindness."

Adam's eyes connected with the eyes of others – a Divine spark. Holding up the mass card we had created, Fr. Thomas pointed out the fitting contrast of the two very different quotes we had chosen, Dr. Seuss ("Don't cry because it's over. Smile because it happened") and the St. Paul quote I referred to earlier, and the picture of my handsome kid, with beautiful eyes and a winning smile. He referred to the things he did, and how he made us laugh... An old soul in a young body – a Soul Shining - a glimpse of Divine love, a spark of God's love...

"Sparks ignite fires!" He inspired the kids there to become aware of their own spark of divine love. "Who are you touching? How are you loving?" He asked. His homily was a tribute to Adam, and his generous life, and in hindsight, so fitting. As my pastor spoke, I was aware and proud of my Spirit-filled boy, my son who, following the theory of Brené Brown, would certainly be counted among those who have lived with their "whole heart." It was amazing (or perhaps not really), how he was inspired to share what Adam would continue to show me over the next years, namely the presence of something alive - the Spirit: in Adam, in me, in all of us.

Inner Being...

What a caterpillar calls the end of the
world we call a butterfly.

Eckhart Tolle

Before Adam died I was reading and growing, and after, naturally, I stopped reading for a long time. Covid shutdowns in March of 2020 gave me the time not only to begin writing but also to start reading, or at least start burning the audible credits again. As I was writing that summer, St. Paul's message to the Galatians and Brené' Brown's research around wholehearted living came together while I was reflecting one day on ideas presented in a new book I had picked up by Eckhart Tolle.

Tolle's words and inspiration accompanied me as I formed a new practice of daily walks during the early weeks of Covid. Working from home cut an hour off of my daily commute, so things like exercise and books found a place in my routines. Even if it was listening rather than reading, *"The Power of Now"* was just the second book I managed to finish and was equally impactful as the first (the Bette Eadie book that had inspired my new perspective around Adam's "purpose").

Eckhart Tolle is a best-selling author. Oprah Winfrey considers him a modern prophet, and they have developed a series of podcasts together. He's met with world leaders like the Dalai Lama and is considered one of the most influential and inspired spiritual teachers alive today. It's hard to believe this if you google him. His appearance suggests a pretty regular, simple guy, but he's legit, and his books have inspired millions. I don't recall how or why this book ended up on my audible cue; it was likely recommended based on previous selections, which might also explain the common themes I found threading them all.

Tolle has a simple message - to live in the present moment, in touch with our Inner Being. We tend to get fixated on what happened in the past, or anxiety about the future, and both cloud what is real - what's right here, right now. Our focus on previous pains or insult or movies we make in our mind of an imagined future, create a false, mind-constructed identity that distracts us from actual reality. If we can go beyond, silencing the noise in our heads, our "real self" inhabits a quiet still place underneath it all, a place of subtle but intense love, joy, and peace. If we can bring ourselves to stay present, aware of what is right here now, so much of the pain we create by harping on the past or worrying about the future disappears. Love and Joy, the essence of our being, become more evident and obvious. *Love, Joy, Peace* ... sound familiar?

Though Tolle is considered a spiritual teacher, he is not aligned with any religion. St. Paul is an ancient Christian disciple and letter writer, Fr. Richard Rohr, a Catholic Franciscan monk, and Dr. Brené Brown is a college professor, researcher, and author. They share a lot "not" in common. But as I wrote over the past spring and summer with *"The Power of Now"* still recent in my mind, I was struck by how much Tolle's ideas, the quote from Galatians, and Brown's guideposts for living wholeheartedly all shared in common. Most amazing was that the realization was sparked by similar themes, messages, and ideas threading the stories, dreams, and experiences I was writing about Adam.

Ok, wait. What? Am I stretching things here? How could any of that incredible wisdom have even a remote connection to Adam, a 15-year-old kid who likely never heard of any of them?

Just hours after the tragedy on November 12, 2017, as I sat alone in my kitchen looking at the clock, I experienced that brief but still vividly recollected Love, Joy, and Peace in reliving the Spirit-filled traits in Adam through brief but explicit memories of his life. Yes, Adam was a normal teenage boy who likely skipped church the very night he died, but he also abounded with all those fruits - saintly in its own right, and so simple. Angst, anxiety, worry, fear, resentment (Tolle's barriers to Consciousness), were not in his repertoire, not even single memories. He got angry, could even hold a short grudge, but it stayed and never overtook him. Much of it was just who he was in his core. He could be a tease, even get in your face, but anyone who knew him would have a hard time recalling a lack of peace, even during an intense game of Minecraft. He was clearly recognized for his own connection to what's real, to his "Inner Being" as Tolle articulates, and his own "Fruits of the Spirit" (according to St. Paul) emanating in his authenticity, calm, resilience, lightheartedness, and laughter; or as Brené Brown might put it, for his own "guideposts" for living with his "whole heart."

And it all came together more perfectly when I decided to transcribe the funeral visitation book.

Dear Naomi,

I was lucky to be friends with Adam since first or second grade and throughout high school. He's meant so many different things to me as we grew up together. When we were young I remember always hanging out with him, Tommy, the Lloyds and all the neighborhood boys playing outside. Adam would always come up with new games for us to play like Survivor and the Nerf wars we had. He was always one of the funniest kids I knew and would give everyone positive energy. I still remember all of us playing in your yard and on the trampoline and going out together on Halloween. Adam never changed his personality in high school and our relationship grew stronger. He was still one of the funniest kids for sure and laughed probably more than anyone else. He was someone I could always count on to cheer up the mood when people were annoyed or sad, and always crack stupid jokes which made everyone laugh. He also would always look out for all of us. He would be the one to reach out to someone who wasn't included or in a bad mood and he was the last person to stab one of us in the back. He would call us out if he knew we were being jerks to each other and would keep us in check. This would lead to some conflict, but in the end he always brought us together. He showed me what I needed to stop doing and what I needed to improve about myself, and still today I see Adam as somewhat of a mentor for me. I'm so lucky to have a friend like him who I know is going to be there for me forever and through anything, which Adam clearly was. I love him and I'm proud to call him one of my brothers. ... and I hope we can all continue to remember Adam as a strong person he was.

Love,

Peter T.

...And a Wordle

Adam's obituary was written by his siblings Billy, Kit, Mindy, JohnPaul, and Jude, plus the girls we call "God siblings," Katie and Lilly Sullivan. We have always been very close with the Sullies. We get together on holidays for a fortifying cocktail visit before going to our real families. I grew up across the street from Emily, the mom, and we became close friends when I was in high school even though she is a few years older. We were at each other's weddings, and the backyards where we have raised our families together almost touch. Our children never had to cross a street to get to each other, and for that reason their home was always a second home for my kids. They could get to one another independently and became inseparable before they remember. The Sullies are like family, so when Doug and I asked Em and James, her husband, to become Jude's Godparents, it made the relationship official, we were "God-family." We consider ourselves related, and so it was natural that they helped write the obituary:

"Adam Martin Brickel passed away suddenly on November 12, 2017. Adam is the son of Naomi Hickey Brickel and Douglas Brickel, and brother of William, Kit, Mindy, Johnny, and Jude. He is also the grandson of his adoring grandmother, Kitty Hickey, and loved by his

many cousins, aunts, uncles, countless friends, and his beloved dog,
Kelly, whom he spent his last moments with.

Adam was a kind, funny, creative, and intelligent person, who had a
charming way of being everyone's best friend. As a sophomore at New
Rochelle High School, Adam was loved by everyone due to his friendly
and charismatic personality, and his way of being unapologetically
himself. An entrepreneurial teen, Adam was known to buy and later
sell designer sneakers. If he wasn't on the computer playing Minecraft,
Adam spent his time doing impersonations, making prank phone calls,
and drinking Starbucks Frappuccinos. We all will miss the color he
brought into our lives every day. There was truly no one like him.

The family will receive friends at the Brickel home on Tuesday (11/14)
and Wednesday (11/15) between the hours of 3PM and 8PM. (Please
park on side streets.)

A Mass of Christian Burial celebrating Adam's life will be held on
Thursday, November 16, 2017 at 12 noon at Saints John & Paul
Church, 280 Weaver Street, Larchmont, NY 10538..."

As shared already, I grew up in and have a large family.
Most of my siblings have settled near where we grew up. We
have raised cousins who enjoy each other, in some cases go to
school together, and have friends in common. Within a square
mile there are literally hundreds of friends from a lifetime,
friends we grew up with, new friends, siblings' friends, parents'
friends, grandparents' friends. Everyone knew Adam's services
would be big and crowded. This was a shocking tragedy in a
cohesive established community.

As we began to make arrangements, I envisioned
standing in line in a funeral home, my kids alongside, Doug
struggling in his illness to stand so long, all of us tired, tense, in
shock, trying to suppress tensions, daunted by a mass of

mourners coming to pay their respects, an unending line of crushed and sad faces coming to say how sorry they all were. I couldn't do it to any of us, and made the decision to let people come and pay respects at our house. I stole the idea from Jewish friends whose shiva services I have attended and found more personal and comforting. The idea of being at home was more intimate, more tolerable. I wanted my family to be sustained by those who came to the house, not have to work.

It was the right decision. Five hours two days in a row was grueling, yet fulfilling. I have no idea how many people came, I heard there were more than a thousand in the church and it felt unending at the house too. But it was comforting to see lifelong friends, and those of my siblings, neighbors, work colleagues, my kids' friends and teachers (some who had or would teach all six) all standing in my dining room. It felt good to have kids come and tell me stories of how Adam had touched their lives, and then see them go hang out with his siblings. It took pressure off to see my husband and offspring surrounded in the comfort and familiarity of their home. I didn't have to worry; they were being well taken care of by the people they most cared about.

I remember a lot of the faces who visited over those two days, but there were so many I had never even met. It was shocking to be presented with a side of Adam I never had any knowledge of, his vast network of friends, and the way he had impacted people. This was a kid who had been so addicted to Minecraft that I worried about his socialization. Whenever he'd gone out, and I asked him who he was with, it was always the same response, "Will, Avery, Peter..." I was stunned to have so many kids in my house, all sharing stories of his kindness, humor, and magnanimity. And so many girls! He had never mentioned a girl's name since he was a little boy playing with

Lili Mae across the street. Now they were pouring through the door and introducing themselves, so many indicating "he was my best friend."

When you go to a wake in a funeral home there is usually a book to sign so the family can recall who came. My sister thought that even though we were doing things differently, this would still be a good idea. She went to our local book store to find something nice that would serve the purpose. The woman working had a wonderful idea. She suggested an attractive, but sturdy and substantial, blank-paged book and some colored pens, to let people visiting share memories of Adam. The book was on the dining room table, and everyone who knew him was encouraged to share a memory. No one could have imagined the treasure it would become, much less the messages it would reveal.

I did not have the strength or courage to open the book for two years. And when I finally did, understandably, I could only read it in short sittings; there was so much, and it was so very beautiful and extremely intense. I had heard immediately from family members who opened it that it was powerful, but when I finally read the words myself, I was still struck by how many people he touched in such meaningful ways - so much more than simple shallow acquaintances.

Beginning the morning after he died, the kids in one of Adam's classes created a memorial, writing messages in sharpie on his desk. The high school eventually donated the desk to our family and, though it still sits prominently in my living room, I noticed that some of what was written was beginning to fade and disappear. I also noticed that letters or notes written after he died, especially those in pencil, were becoming difficult to read.

Desperate not to lose any more precious memories - my last remaining pieces of him - to the passing of time, I decided to create an electronic copy of the funeral memory book so the messages could be preserved. During Covid, I sat over many days reading kids' memories into the dictation feature in Google Docs. I didn't include everything. Some had simply signed the book to indicate their presence or expressed condolences when they did not know Adam directly. There were also some others that were impossible to read or decipher. I got much of it though, and it was all in one 20-something-page - incredibly rich - document.

As I reread and recited literally hundreds of treasures written by people who knew him, I was moved by their memories. So many wrote of his kindness, his smile, his laugh and huge happiness, how he cherished friendship and family - even blurring the lines and mixing it together in referring to each other as "brotha." There were beautiful messages articulating his alertness to others, their situations and experience, and of his authenticity, evidenced in an attention to the importance of being real and true, and his calling out people he considered "fake." I began to perceive obvious and discrete themes threading it, similar to what had resonated in St. Paul's Spiritual "Fruits," the qualities of being connected with "Inner Being" identified by Eckhart Tolle, and Brené Brown's "Guideposts" for living wholeheartedly.

My work and the pursuit of a master's degree has provided the opportunity to gain a peripheral familiarity with academic research. Thematic analysis is a process used to identify themes or patterns within qualitative data (i.e. written responses, interview transcripts, etc.). As a trainer who's led workshops for families and professionals, I have also worked with polling and survey tools in sessions I've led. A "wordle" is an interactive and entertaining software that creates a word cloud from input responses or text, visually representing the frequency of words used in responses, with more frequently used words appearing larger or more bold than others. In my amateur brain, a wordle is a kind of rough and basic qualitative research data "coding" tool. As I sat there over days creating this new document, I became intrigued by the idea of using such a tool with the content I'd transcribed to see objectively what might pop out. I was curious, so I took what I had completed, and I cut and pasted it into a free word cloud generating software I found on the internet. It was amazing.

Of course, the biggest word was Adam, large and bold in the middle of the "cloud". What struck and inspired me, though, was the prominence of certain words representing his observed values, words like, "nicest," "kind," "spirit," "smile," "bro," "laugh," "light," "easy," "family," "heart." The messages were right there in the kids' words, in what they had remembered about Adam, what they chose to memorialize. I can't say it was scientific, and there were lots of "RIP's" and "sorry's" to convey the condolences. But there was something real. It motivated me to be more scientific and apply what I had learned about qualitative research to actually code the data. I finished transcribing the book and began to go through each memory, identifying and highlighting themes. I'm certainly no expert and I can't vouch for the validity of my process (I'm also clearly predisposed to researcher bias). Nevertheless, I feel pretty confident that I pinpointed the main concepts threading it all. They were consistent, repetitive and obvious, to the point that it would be hard to confuse.

Something that also stood out and impacted me was the tone of the kids' memories compared to those of the adults. Generally, the kids seemed to express more upbeat, thankful, "happy-that-it-happened" messages as opposed to the more condolence focused, sympathetic, "sad-that-it-ended" messages of the adults. And "#'s", the kids used so many hashtags! One in particular came up in a few places. "#Adam'sWorld" was used by kids who seemed to share his class schedule or at least a number of classes that fall, where I deduced he must have held court frequently. (Class clown is a genetic attribute Adam clearly inherited.) There were also frequent Adam-related hashtags on social media to mark anniversaries, birthdays, important days, or simply just used by friends missing him.

Hashtags are this generation's mechanism for summarizing, categorizing, and focusing attention - kind of like their own laypersons' thematic analysis tool. As I continued to write, read and reflect on what was in those pages, hashtags seemed an appropriate and suitable way to bring light to Adam's lights, and highlight the important messages, which, I started to think, might be part of his "purpose."

I only knew Adam for a short time but the impact he had on people was truly beautiful and evident even from the first time I saw him. Just last weekend I hung out with Adam, as soon as he walked in, everyone's spirits were lifted because he brought his wonderful smile and mood that everyone loved. When I think of him, his everlasting positive attitude and love of everyone he met stays with me.
  -Calvin J.

Brené Brown, Richard Rohr, Eckhart Tolle, and St. Paul are awesome. The messages in their work are timeless, and for me they have been life altering. Each played a critical role in restoring my happiness after this tragedy. I share their books and give them out as gifts because I want to spread the wealth and bring their powerful messages to people. And, while this is difficult to write, and may be uncomfortable to read (perhaps even feel offensive to some), it's real for me: Adam's death - or more appropriately, his life, highlighted more intensely by his abrupt sudden death - was the harshest, most horrible ... and best thing that ever happened to me. Crazy. Incredible. True.

But I'm in my 50's, teetering on the cusp of irrelevant. ... And something that's become clear is that Adam has his own messages to share, perhaps equally important, and more meaningful to a younger generation who communicates in hashtags. I believe it's the young people who are going to need to get us out of this seemingly hopeless mess of times we are in. Perhaps hashtags (and their own language from the texts and snaps on his phone), inspired by young people, in their observations of what was important and meaningful in a boy who clearly impacted them, a kid who brought joy, peace and "his everlasting positive attitude" to the people he touched in his short life - might provide a framework. Why not let Adam share his own message, speaking through what I found right there in the "data" - the pieces of himself he left with those kids, and they generously offered back in their thoughtful and heartfelt inscriptions in "The Book."

Adam's Hashtags ...

#Adam'sWorld

Hashtags for Livin' Yzy

(How to live your best life)

#ODEFUN (Happiness and gratitude)

#KTF (Faith)

#CWG (Family/Friendship)

#IGotU (Kindness/Attention to others)

#FAKE (Authenticity)

#YUTIGHT (Acceptance - It's all good)

#fromAdam

#ODEFUN

I had Adam in all my classes for 2 years straight and not once have I ever seen him without a smile on his face.... he made everyone smile and no matter how many times I corrected him he would always yell out Ja-mow-kee with the biggest smile. He was the best person I've ever met. he was PERFECT in every way.   I really love that guy:) #ADAM'sWORLD Love, Jimonee G.

The first and most obvious theme that emerged in my unqualified analysis was Adam's happiness. I was tempted not to start with it, it seemed too basic and obvious. Personally, I would have preferred to begin with the messages connected to faith or spirit. Those things resonate more for me. But the archive spoke, and the more I went back to "The Book" - to the kids' actual words, Adam's actual impact in their lives - the more I couldn't deny "Joy - Fun - Happy." If I was going to represent Adam, stay true to the data and the messages the book generated, it had to begin there. So much was written about his smile and the way it lit up a room, by far the most defining feature people recognized. The word "smile" appeared over 110 times, and "laugh" an additional 40. When you added words with similar meaning, like the LMAOs and LOLs, etc., it was hundreds ...

Adam.... always had a smile on his face. When I would see him in the halls he looked so happy to see you, as if there was no one else in that hall. He was always so fun to be with.... You couldn't help but laugh if he was laughing. ~ Kelsey F.

... Obvious enough to indicate that Adam prioritized being happy, the kids prioritized that quality, and he was "ODE FUN."

Not a day has gone by where I haven't thought about Adam. When I think about him there's truly only positive things to think of. When the thought has popped into my head I always imagined his famous and very captivating smile. Although it's just a smile I feel there's a deeper meaning behind it, it represents how he was a happy person and had a sunny personality. When I think of him I think of all the great memories we have together, the memories I will carry for the rest of my life. Adam was very important to me and I treasure every moment we had together. ...

Love,

Shane

Gratitude

Adam, I know you've probably gotten a million thank yous by now, here's a million and one. Thank you so so much. Thank you for being a beacon of light that would always brighten my day. Thank you for always flashing your blinding smile at me. Thank you for all the laughs we shared. Thank you for spending lunch with me. Thank you for suffering through social studies with me. I'm so sorry that you're gone but I'm also so happy that I got to spend time with you. I cherish every moment I've spent with you and I'm so grateful I got to have you in my life. I love you so much and I'll miss you every day
XOXO, Asia 🖤

~

A part of me wishes that each and every second of those last moments with him - before I left him forever - were more vivid, and that I had possessed the presence of mind to mentally record it more deliberately. I encountered many of the lights Adam offered me after his death without enough vigilance. I knew in the moment that they were important, either in their finality or incredible beauty, and often wished days later that I had written things down so I didn't lose them. That's kind of how I feel about those final moments. While it's perfectly explicable that the trauma would have clouded things, I still wish I had more. Even so, what I am left with is a beautiful blessing I treasure.

I don't know if there was anyone around me, nurses or hospital staff, as I went back into him for one last goodbye. Johnny had gone in alone and come back out, and I think Amy and Kirsty had as well. The image I carry is of me and Adam. Just us. He is there lying peacefully. My memory is not fully accurate because the shirt I recollect him wearing is one I still have and cherish. He could not have been in it since I never got those things back. It was quiet. He looked content, somehow not absent, very different from the dreadful horror on the street shortly before. I felt uneasy, not sure what to do and uncomfortable in my ignorance. I walked over and bent to embrace and hold him. He had matured in the months prior. I have found it a gift that I was able to hold him that last time as a man; it's enabled me to relate to him in an adult role. When I communicate with him now, I talk about grown-up things, adult problems, rather than protect him as a mom is inclined to do with children. I feel the liberty to lay heavy things on him and keep it real.

I have shared this next experience with few people, my therapist, maybe my mom, almost no one else; mostly because I worry that people might not believe it, suspect I'm being fake, dramatic, or a Pollyanna.

As I held him, I was flooded with emotion. One might expect or be inclined to picture a broken anguished mother - agony, desperation, despair - but that's not what happened at all. Instead, I was overcome with gratitude, "Thank you"s and gratefulness, simultaneously to Adam for the beauty he had bestowed on me, my family, and the world, and also to God for letting it all be.

"Thank you!" Out loud and expressive. For every moment of his life, for the funny things he did to make us laugh, for the radar he kept himself under, never causing me worry. Even acting the typical teenager, he kept it from my attention in a way most teens often don't.

"Thank you!" Again. For his passionate emotional love for me as a baby and toddler, and as he grew for his siblings. For the fleshy fat pads on his hands and feet that we all loved to chomp on when he was little, that gave him the nickname "Chub," a term of affection used only for him.

"Thank you!" Emotional joyful sobbing. For the curve balls he threw at me, challenging how I might be thinking or reacting in a situation or family dynamic. For walking the dog when I assumed he hadn't. For being a better person than I ever seemed to give him credit for.

"Oh my God, Thank you!" For his physical beauty and his opaque hair, his face, the dark Mediterranean skin, unique among his siblings and cousins in our big Irish family.

"Oh Adam, Thank you!!" For being homesick the summer before on his trip to Spain, and Facetiming every day. For the frequent texts over the fall requesting bagels on my way home from work, and my contentment in being able to stop to please him, during a time I was worried he might need my attention.

"Oh Adam. Oh Adam. Thank you!" For the laughter, prank phone calls, our mischief together, entertaining friends and cousins. How he made people laugh with his 'twerking,' loud singing outbursts, and dialect imitations.

"Thank you! Oh, my God, Oh Adam, Thank you!"

Incredibly, I experienced nothing but gratitude, no loss, no regrets, no remorse for anything I could have done differently, no anger at God. I guess it's hard to be sad when you're focused on so much wonderful. I was not noble or strong, but rather, raw and exposed. It rushed out unfiltered and completely, beautifully, appropriate but unexpected given the situation, like a rum punch in a hurricane, somehow and somewhat fitting, but unanticipated in the duress. It was an incredible grace, a gift from God. Or perhaps it was Adam's parting gift, he always preferred happy to melancholy or distress. My first experience of his death, and all I could say was "Thank you"!!

Certainly a miracle, and a gift of faith.

Long before Adam died, my friend Laurie shared the concept of a gratitude journal. Apparently, people who note things for which to be grateful are happier. She had suggested it to a young adult relative and told me about it one day when we were out walking. I never started one myself, but was always intrigued. I recall suggesting it to Kit or Billy during a time of stress. Laurie and I do not see each other often; but we share an affinity for meditation, self-help, and well-being, so when we do, we often circle back to those topics. During Covid she called to catch up. She told me about Mooji, a Jamaican spiritual teacher, thinking I might appreciate his meditations on inner being. I did. In those first months of shutdowns I took long walks and often stopped at my parish chapel to pray. I frequently listened to Mooji to bring me into presence.

On Mother's Day right in the midst of Covid, I walked down to be with Adam at his resting place by the lakes at the High School. The weather was lovely. I listened to happy music over airpods as I walked. When I got there, I sat on the bench overlooking the water and was struck by the beauty of the day, the surroundings, and a feeling of closeness to him. I decided to revel in it more deliberately, and opened my phone to search YouTube for a short meditation to bring me even further into awareness. The one I found was a Mooji meditation for "challenging times," recently recorded to offer solace during Covid. And what was the focus for such anxious times? Gratitude. Over and over he kept repeating "Thank you." Thank you for health, for the ability to sit or stand, for family, friends, food, health, existence, Life... Thank you, God. Thank you, Heavenly Father!

Mooji's thank you's pulled me back to that night, to my last minutes and the joy I felt as I thanked God and Adam for his beauty and beautiful life. I thanked Adam again, not only for the love and happiness he had generously bestowed that night, but also for what he was offering me again now, on Mother's Day. My eyes filled with tears. I wept, not in sadness, but in thanks and joy. I sat there on Adam's bench, deeply aware and connected with his presence, and was overwhelmed as I recognized so much around me that was good.

Adam is generous. He gives me a gift on every holiday, and for Mother's Day it is often more obvious. This year in the middle of Covid it was different. It was not a new friend or the tattoo with his ashes that she arranged, nor was it a special friend's unexpected visit, as in years prior. Subtly and understatedly, it was actually more grandiose and transformational, yet might have been missed completely had I not been present and tuned in. As I sat there with him by the lakes weeping, I suddenly understood the joy-inspiring power of "Thank you," the power to transform what might otherwise be a sad holiday during Covid to a day of light and beauty, and a huge smile; and the power to transform a mother's devastating final goodbye into a cherished and beautiful memory. So simple, and so powerful.

I have incorporated gratitude into my daily 20-minute meditation ritual and now allocate ten minutes to simply thanking God for things. We take so much for granted, like the warm shower, the sun coming up, or even a cup of coffee. I try to be more conscious of all of it now.

"Thank you, Father, for the sunlight."

"Thank you for this wonderful awesome ocean."

"Thank you for Kit's call, and Mindy's Facetime."

"Thank you for Jude's beautiful curls, for my friend's kindness, that memory that just made me laugh, this beautiful fireplace, the sun on my face, my cool car, Billy's gentle way, that smile that just lifted me, bacon of the month, his amazing insight, her cute comment, the guy who was willing to tattoo Adam's ashes and Emily who made it happen, that ripe mango, the perfect oyster, JohnPaul's understated smile, yellowfin tuna, the squirrel building its nest each morning, that work colleague's passion, the kindness of others, this wine, that tequila, the sparkle of the snow, my overjoyed dog ..."

When I stop and become present, pay attention and appreciate, simple things I would typically take for granted become great and provide joy - the coffee actually tastes better! It's hard to feel grumpy or sad when you are mindful of the things you appreciate. When we're grateful we can't help but be happy, focused on the things that bring us joy, maintaining our presence and awareness of it all. We're less available for spinning off into our head and the worry and anxious things we create there. It sounds simple (Adam's messages seem to follow that formula), but gratitude, a genuine thank you, is not just good manners. It's also life altering, happiness inspiring, and transformational.

Yes, Universe, "Thank you!"

And Adam, "Thank you, too

Smile Because It Happened

When you were in school you were smiling. When you were outside of school you were smiling. Now you're in heaven smiling. Rayyen S. 🖤

For Adam's funeral I wore the appropriate black dress, but refused to accessorize with the boring beige scarf that had been pre-selected for me by the lifelong dear friends and family who coordinated everything. There were decisions I had to make in the preparations, and for these they consulted me; but others not, and they were just done. I'm not into dress up, so what I would wear was a decision and tasks that were filled in. Except the scarf. As I dressed that morning into everything that had been laid out perfectly, the brown scarf just felt so, well, brown. And not Adam at all.

My favorite color is pink. I love pink because it is the color of bubble gum, cotton candy, and peonies. Adam liked pink too, probably for the same reasons (except the flowers), so wearing it seemed appropriate for a Mass commemorating his life and his happy, candy-filled world. I wore a pink pashmina and left the brown scarf on the hanger. When I came downstairs, my mom started to "suggest" the beige, but no one else dared (or perhaps cared). This was a decision I was going to make. I got a text during the funeral from my friend, Cathy. "Of course, you are in pink." It fit, perfectly.

The music was beautiful, I picked each song deliberately, all moving and powerful. And then there was the eulogy. Eulogies are tough. Needing to navigate the fine line to keep it personal but appropriate for church, the intense and acute grief, and the fact that, after all, it's someone close, poses a challenge even for the most adept, experienced, and diplomatic. In this case, Adam's big sister, Kit, would deliver it.

She was quite determined, but admittedly how it would play out in the moment concerned me. Adam and Kit were so close, her grief so raw. How could my broken 22-year-old have the strength to stand up and deliver a speech at her precious brother's funeral? I left it in Adam's hands. We also agreed that her cousin, Dana, and God-sister, Katie, would stand with her, just in case.

Although Kit is close with all of her siblings, she and Adam had a special bond and shared something unique. Kit cherishes family and actively nurtures the relationships with all of us, siblings, parents, her grandmother, cousins, and extended family alike. Since, due to his illness, Doug has been locked down in his nursing facility and unable to see any of us in Covid, she's remembered to send him a letter or card every week. She is the one who stays connected with his family.

After Adam died, we decided we would strengthen and feed our own relationship. Though I set a weekly reminder to call her on Tuesday mornings on my way to work, she's the one who's always followed through. While I'm likely to get in the car and immediately get distracted with the office and what awaits me there, the phone always rings at 8:20 with Kit on the other end. When my 85-year-old mom was invited to her grandniece's wedding, but reluctant to make the trip alone, Kit jumped at the opportunity to accompany her and meet her distant cousins. She Facetimes daily with her sister Mindy, facilitates the sibling group text thread, and coordinates presents for me on holidays and birthdays from all of the other siblings. During Covid, Kit organized the family Zoom and online game night. She is creative, caring, conscientious, smart, friendly, and fun. And I have never been so proud as I was watching a beautiful, poised, articulate woman, my own strong daughter, speak poignantly to a crowd of a thousand. She captured Adam so perfectly that many reacted saying how much they felt like they knew him:

"For those of you who don't know me, I'm Kit, Adam's older sister.

"If you could all please be silent for a second and just think to yourself of a single word that describes Adam. It's hard isn't it? Even though I can't read minds, I know you are all thinking of something completely different. And that's the beauty of Adam, he was so incredibly special that there is a never-ending list of words we could use to describe him. He was smart, clever, kind, outgoing, compassionate, and downright hilarious. The list goes on and on.

"I want to share a few memories that I've held close to my heart about Adam and I think everyone should hear. To start off, I remember Adam being an absolute nightmare of a toddler. He would climb out of his crib all the time, bang his head against the wall when he didn't get what he wanted (really there is a period of about a year in pictures where he had a bruised cheek). He even had the nerve to scream about not having a blanket that choked him, and we had to make it into his beloved BooBoo Bear just to appease him. I think he was just in shock that my mom sprung another kid on us, even though she swore that after Adam she was done.

"So being the devilish preteen I was, I figured that Adam would appreciate some love. I could get him on my good side, and Jude, the

baby, already got enough attention. So, I put him on my lap one day and said, "You know you're my favorite right?" He turned around and gave me a weird look and said, "Really?" And all I said was, "Yup," and he was convinced. And I guess so was I. From then on Adam and I had such an incredible, unique bond.

"Another beautiful thing about Adam is how he touched the lives of everyone he met, and watching him grow up, I know that he shared a special bond with so many of you. For my grandmother, like most grandmothers, he was someone that never really ate enough, but had such a good heart that it didn't even matter. For my parents, he was a breeze (after his early years of course), someone they never had to worry about, and someone that brought light into the family. For Billy, he was a form of entertainment, I hope none of you recall "The Adam Show" - pretty sure Billy was the one who fed into that the most. For Mindy, he was a menace, but a menace in the most loving way, I mean you have to build character somehow right? For Johnny, a best friend, a gym buddy, a partner in crime. They were so close that he'd even obnoxiously call all of his friends for rides and food. I heard Johnny tell him to stop once, but I'm sure none of you minded because, once again, you all had very special bonds with him. For Jude, he was a role model, someone that was going to buy him a pair of Yeezys someday, when he finally made some money off those stupid shoes. For Kelly, he was a dad, sometimes a fellow "borker" and someone to snuggle with every night. For his older cousins, aunts and uncles he was a complete obnoxious goofball who would pull stupid pranks. For his younger cousins, he was a best friend, a protector. During summers in Westhampton, I remember him orchestrating intricate sandcastles, or taking people into town to get candy, making sure everyone got enough before he would get any. He was always so kind that way. To his friends, real or on Minecraft, he was a fellow ding-dong-ditcher, a "Yeezy gang member," someone that would go to McDonald's with

108

you at 2AM at the drop of a hat (sorry I'm breaking my promise about not telling anyone about that), and a true companion. To his classmates and teachers he was a comedian, someone that made everyone laugh and smile, doing different accents or making stupid jokes. The list is endless. For me Adam, or should I say "Chub" or "Laquisha" was someone I always felt the need to protect. I remember taking him for long walks and drives when he was upset, because the second oldest and the second youngest have to stick together, right?

"He could get me to do whatever he wanted, and I mean whatever. As soon as I got my license, it was always 'Kiiiiit, could you take me to Starbucks?' 'Kiiiiit, let's go to Stop & Shop to get cookie mix!' 'Kiiiitt, can we drive to the city to sit in a Dunkin' Donuts so I have a better chance of getting a ridiculous $500 pair of shoes?' The answer was always 'yes' and if it wasn't 'yes' the first time, he would find a way to get me to say 'yes,' even if I had been asleep for two hours, or looking like a complete mess. He even got me to sit on a computer for 3 hours to preorder a pair of shoes while he was in Spain. Don't worry, he gave me a full detailed lesson about how to use the 'bot' he bought to bypass the system. Even so, unfortunately, I somehow managed to not get the shoes.

"I'm sure most of you know this, but Adam was definitely a 'sassy one.' One of my favorite stories was when his Spanish teacher called our house one day because he wanted to express to my mom how much he loved having him in his class, and how he would change his accent depending on who he was talking to. I remember even the day he died, he made me drive him to the grocery store to get a job application because he was broke from spending all his money on the stupid shoes. We were just sitting in the parking lot at Stop & Shop, and he goes, 'Nah this 'fit' won't work, we gotta come back tomorrow.' And I was like, 'Excuse me your what?' And he just rolled his eyes and goes, 'My outfit.'

"I think Adam is the only person who would think like that.

"Because of his sassy front, I don't think he expressed how much he cared about each and every one of you, and if he did it was probably in some random, inappropriate accent, but he definitely showed his love through his everyday actions. He provided comic relief, baked goods (with assistance from the Sullivan's, constantly asking them for cupcake holders), was a peacemaker, someone who saw color and culture and difference and accepted it in a way that I don't think I have seen anyone do before, a little brother to not just immediate family, and a friend to all.

"For me, I remember him sending me stupid one words texts for ZERO reason when I was away at school, posing for pictures with me, bringing me back a thirty euro stuffed ham instead of a stuffed animal when he went away abroad, making Johnny drive him to the mall just so he could get me expensive macaroons for my birthday, because I had bought him cupcakes for his a week prior, writing in his second grade journal something along the lines of, 'I have 5 siblings but Kit likes me the best,' Facetiming me every day while he was away in Spain, or calling me out for being ridiculous. I knew how much he cared, and how much he appreciated me and loved me just by these little things.

"I encourage you all to think of these little things as I did.

"A week ago two students from New Rochelle also passed away in a tragic accident, and after hearing about this he said to my other brother Johnny, "If I die I wouldn't want anyone to be sad." So, I encourage you all to try your best not to be sad because it's what he wanted. Also, I'm sure in a few days if you're feeling sad, you'll hear his sassy voice in your head saying something like, 'Why you being such a grump? I told you I don't want you to be sad and you ackin sad!!'

"To end, I just wanted to say that Adam was the light of my life and I'm sure he was the same for all of you. Don't worry, I know that light *will continue to shine through just in a different way because after all, the second oldest and the second youngest have got to stick together, right Adam?"*

~

... "If I die, I don't want anyone to be sad." Yes, Adam really did say that to his brother days before he died. What did he know? Was there some sort of premonition, a subconscious awareness?

On November 4, 2017 (just eight days before Adam's own death), early on a Saturday morning, there was a terrible accident. A speeding car driving down Route 1 in Mamaroneck, NY (two towns over), drove into a garbage truck that was making a turn. The road was shut down. You knew it was really bad when you heard helicopters. There were deaths. It made the news. I'm news oblivious and don't watch TV or read newspapers. I only look for stuff online when there is a major snowstorm or hurricane impending, a pandemic hits, or I hear helicopters. I learned about the accident immediately and was shaken. Route 1 was closed all day. As a major thoroughfare, it is a big deal for it to be shut down at all, much less all day. There have been just a few times in my life that I even recall this happening, some in which I peripherally knew victims.

Here two young men, close in age to my own boys, had died. I was pained for their mothers. I too had teenagers, they drive too fast. Boys can be such risk takers and too frequently underestimate their mortality. It could just as easily have been my sons. My heart ached. Every mother's worst nightmare.

The following Monday night we were at the kitchen table eating dinner. It was Doug, Adam, Johnny, Mindy, Jude, and me. JohnPaul and Adam started talking about the accident. The two young men who died were boys from New Rochelle,

Omar and Rolando, cousins. Rolando had graduated from New Rochelle High School and Omar was still a student there. My boys knew them. Omar had shared a class with Mindy and JohnPaul two years before.

"Mom," Johnny said, "That kid Omar was a really nice kid. Remember that class me and Mindy took together that year? He was in that class with us. And Mom, he was seriously like the nicest kid to Mindy. He did the nicest things to her."

Mindy has a rare genetic disorder which manifests in characteristics of autism and a mild intellectual disability, along with other physical and medical conditions. Among other things, including a beautiful voice and pure heart, she has struggled all her life with learning and social challenges, medical issues that required long hospital stays, two brain surgeries, a near death crisis of her own, epilepsy, and just being different. Because her disabilities interfered with her learning and behavior, special segregated classes in other schools were offered, but I was never comfortable with the idea of different busses, different schools, or even separate classes from her siblings and the other neighborhood kids. Being surrounded by so many who knew and would stand by her provided built in socialization - and protection. I had always advocated for her to be integrated and attend the same schools and regular classes as much as possible, even in high school. Middle and high school years are challenging for kids who fit in perfectly; but for kids with disabilities and differences, they can be brutal. Mindy's experience was no exception. While she was blessed to meet wonderful inclusive kids, sing in a nationally recognized choir, travel to Japan and Florida to perform, participate in two plays, and make real friends in her six years at New Rochelle High School, she also encountered mean kids, isolation, and bullying.

So, when I heard examples of kindness from kids like Omar, it lifted my heart.

Somehow, that dinner table conversation led to follow up between Adam and Johnny which prompted him to say *that* line, "If I die, I don't want anyone to be sad." Something so strange, just days before his own death. It's what prompted me to choose this quote from Dr. Seuss for the back of the mass card a week later, "Don't cry because it's over, smile because it happened."

That night, after the conversation at the dinner table, I was scrolling through Facebook and came across a GoFundMe page for the boys' funerals. I had never met either of them or their families, but I made a donation, feeling fortunate for this small way to thank Omar for his generous life. It felt just a little bit good that, although I could not (yet) fathom his mother's pain over the loss of her pure hearted son and wished I could somehow rewind it, I could at least offer a minute comfort, small thanks for raising a good boy with the courage to be kind to Mindy.

I'm not sure whether Adam's words were a premonition, or just one of life's ironies. I also never imagined that Omar's mother and I would join the club to which no mother seeks membership, in the same monthly billing cycle. It's an expensive club and, fortunately for those not in it, exclusive. But the significance of the coincidences is too great to simply discount without at least considering an underlying message, and how one might try to live it.

… Maybe as simple as a happy smile or kind word.

White Beemer

It was 2:15 a.m. on the morning of December 21, 2019, exactly two years, one month, and 8 days, almost to the hour, after coming from the hospital after Adam's death. My phone was ringing; it was the police.

Why the precise detail? When you're the parent of teenagers and get a call in the middle of the night with the police on the other end, you brace yourself for what is coming. Calls from the police are gut-wrenching, and not uncommon with teenagers, especially my boys. The doorbell is worse, entailing a walk from bed down the stairs to the front door. That's time enough for everything possible to spin through your head, including the lurking potential that it's not about the kids at all, but a violent criminal at the door. I steadied myself, trying to determine if I could handle whatever it was. I remember thinking I had already been through the worst and survived, I would handle it.

Situations like this used to fill me with agitation and angst. I used to battle regular bouts of anxiety. Since Adam died, I rarely experience it at all. He's rubbed off on me. Now in such instances, I'm graced with a "no matter what, it's going to be ok" response. I've experienced hell and will deal with whatever is in front of me. There's no other option. I still get adrenaline rushes and upset if the circumstances warrant, but I possess an 'in control' feeling I never knew before Adam died.

Fortunately, I learned quickly that all were alive and safe. The police knew our family and were empathetic. It turned out that Johnny had taken my car to pick up his friend Ish and had been in an accident. I rushed to the scene. He had hit ice, literally launched from the road, through a small bush (threading a large tree and telephone pole), into a driveway, and up against a wall supporting front stairs. My car was not ok, but Johnny was. I examined the scene and knew that Adam had been on his shoulder. *"Merry Christmas, Mom!"*

One of the officers on the scene had been there, so they all knew about Adam and our roles the night of his death. I had a hard time containing my emotion when I saw what could have been and began to cry. I'm grateful to live in such a community. They understood my reaction, the resurfacing trauma, and were compassionate.

The car was totaled. It was my three-year-old forest green Honda HRV. I loved that car. Losing it was both an inconvenience and sad in itself. But I had a really nice Christmas that year, thankful for what wasn't. After the holidays, I would get a check for the assessed value of the car, minus the deductible. I decided to put it towards a new car and did some research. The Hyundai Kona was a sporty new model with good reviews and cool electronics. I haggled with dealerships all over the Hudson Valley and was then able to negotiate a comparable price with the dealership in New Rochelle. I was excited.

I went to do the final paperwork at the dealership. As I walked down the street that January afternoon, I passed our auto body guy, Ted, who was pulling out of his dealership. Yes, with so many teenage drivers one acquires a personal auto body guy. He's been with the family through a lot of wrecks. I trust him;

he's taken care of our family and makes me laugh and smile. He drove the antique Rolls Royce for my niece's wedding. He and Doug used to love to chat for hours. He would do anything to help me, even unrelated to cars. We waved "hello." Two hours later, after dark, and after closing the deal on my new Hyundai Kona, I walked past him again on the return. This time he was outside and came over to talk to me.

"What's up gorgeous?" He said, just the way he always does.

"I just bought myself a new car!" I responded with pride and excitement.

"You bought a car from someone but Uncle Ted???"

"Yes, I wanted a new car, not a used one. If I'd wanted a used car I would have come to you!" I replied without defensiveness.

"I do new cars too. What'd you get?"

"I got a brand-new Kona. I'm psyched. It's a cool car. And I negotiated a good price."

"Well whatever you negotiated, I coulda got you, at minimum, $500 less with my buyers license"

"Oh jeeze. Don't tell me that, Ted. You're gonna wreck my excitement. I did a lot of research. The Kona is a great car."

"It's a nice car, but you know what darling? As soon as you drive it off the lot it's going to be worth nothing. Unlike this beauty." And he pointed to a white BMW mini SUV. I was unimpressed.

"You really don't know me Ted. That car does nothing for me. I wouldn't want it. It's not me," I said truthfully.

"Hey, how's that sister of yours? How's she doing? Ya know, you and your sister, you know what? You have nothing in common. You know that?"

"Ummm. What?" I didn't know where he was going with this.

"She would never want that Kona. She'd have some sense and want this car."

"We're definitely different, but I wouldn't say we have nothing in common, Ted. She'd probably prefer that car, you're right, but I don't. Cars do nothing for me. Seriously, I don't ever want to drive a car like that."

"Really. You two - nothing in common, you know that? It's like you're not even related. Do you like her? Do you speak to her?"

"Ted! Yes! Of course I like her. You're nuts!"

"Do you talk to her? Like every day? Like do you ever call her on the phone?"

"Well not every day, but yes, we speak to each other. Shut up, Ted. You're crazy!"

"Ok, well, I tell you what then, can you pick up that phone and call her right now so she can talk some sense into you?? Really! Nothing in common, you too. I can't believe it... But listen, I don't want to wreck your excitement. Tell me, how's my man, Doug? I haven't seen you guys since the last car. I miss my friend. I can talk to him for hours!"

We went inside to talk. He was sad to hear of Doug's decline. "I love that guy. He is the nicest!" He asked how we were all holding up after Adam. Somehow, he knows everything. He knew all the details of Adam's death.

Our discussion returned to the car. He asked more questions, pricing, financing, servicing, etc. Then he offered me the Beemer with a year of free service for less than the price of the Kona. We looked up the comp values. It was an offer I couldn't refuse. He would back into the tax and that would be the price. The car would be in my driveway the following day by 5pm with everything taken care of. I walked away from the other deal. No Kona.

On Friday when I got in from work, the car was in my driveway. Ted was waiting for me. I will never go to anyone else. Ted comes and picks up our cars when they need something. He comes by for anything else I need. I love Ted!

I took a spin, and was excited to get up the next morning when, with no work, I could learn my way around my new fancy car: figure out the systems, connect my phone, coordinate my music, etc. I rushed through my morning coffee, eager to go play. It was a bright sunny day and I went out and walked around it. Not bad. I sat in the front seat and pushed the ignition switch. The leather seats felt nice. Maybe I could get used to this whole nice car thing.

I started to explore the electronics, "Connect new phone." There was no list of devices to connect to. Of course there wasn't. While it would have annoyed me to see a list of names in my new car, the fact that one in particular was missing made my heart sink. When someone had borrowed my HRV and connected their own device, I would need to reconnect my phone the next time I drove it, selecting from the list of previously connected devices. The first device listed was always "Adam's IPhone." It had remained some sort of comfort, like a piece of him still there even after two years. Now, my new car, while a snazzy fresh start, came with this secondary loss. My excitement was overshadowed by this further separation, and all I could do was sit in my driveway, in my fancy new car, and cry.

"Mom, really? I mean seriously, it's a brand new Beemer. You're being really dumb." It is always amazing how I feel him, hear the conversation; it's not like a dream or vision, but a presence, an interactive conversational, feeling presence.

"You're right, Adam. It's a new car. I should be excited, happy, grateful." It was a few days before my birthday. Relish it. I redirected my sadness, put on the radio, put the car in reverse and pulled out. I turned up the music really loud. It felt good! I could get used to nice cars. I remembered my Spotify account for which I had just paid up for the commercial free version. I'd connect and get my money's worth.

I pulled over, set it up, selected "Daily Mix 1," a list created for me based on my listening habits, and turned it up louder. Whatever song came on first I wasn't into and I could just skip it. The next song came on: "Soulshine" by the Allman Brothers. The song Adam had told me was ours, with its own incredible story (see chapter with same name). I pulled into a parking lot and I cranked it up. I started to cry, and laugh, feeling him so strongly. He chuckled.

"Beemer or Kona, Mom? Really?? Uhhhh...how about this, mom. Kona?? Seriously? No! How about, ummmm, No! Happy Birthday, Mom! Enjoy your new ride! Be Happy!"

Like any other kid, or his dad the year I got the new vacuum, he gave me the gift he thought I should want, that he would want. Let's face it, a white Beemer is the perfect match for a spanking new clean pair of fresh Yeezys.

You know what, Adam? I'm in. I cherish every mile.

#KTF

Hey Adam, So last Sunday, you sat in the same spot at the kitchen table where I am currently writing this. Billy was fighting with Kit about why he had to go to church but she didn't. We both just sat there, quietly & awkwardly. And I think in your head, somewhere deep down, you knew you were gonna make us all go to church, including me! Maybe it was your last prank on them and all of us, but I feel so lucky that I got the chance to see you right before you were taken from us. On the back of the program for your mass, there was something that said, "Death is nothing at all, I have only slipped away into the next room." That's kinda what I feel has happened. I never got the chance to sit down and talk with you for a while, either you, or Billy & I slipped away into the next room, but I was lucky enough to see you and talk with you enough that I can easily see all the love and joy that everyone saw within you that just couldn't stay in. See you in the next room, Adam.   *~ Christian*

Before Adam died, we said 'Grace before Meals' at our kitchen table every night at dinner. It was always prompted by Adam (evidenced by our lack of consistency since). Food on my fork, halfway to my mouth, Adam's look of feigned indignation creeping into my peripheral vision, "Grace???" he'd interject before the bite could be taken. I was never quite sure whether he was just making fun. Nonetheless, we gave thanks to God each night for our food and blessings, all because of Adam.

"KTF" (Keep The Faith) = The awareness of our Divine nature and connection to something much bigger!

A letter to Adam's grandmother, Kitty:

Dear Mrs. Hickey:

Hello, this is Aviva, Cathy's daughter, and I'm 16 years old.

Today, I had a piano audition for a piano competition, where I played Clair de Lune by Debussy in front of two judges.

While practicing before they called me up to the audition room, I decided to offer up my whole piece for Adam.

For the little I have heard of Adam from friends, I understood that he was a wonderful boy who lived every moment of life with joy and love, truly living in the present moment. When I played my piece, I thought of him, and I played my heart out, putting love and meaning into every note.

Having competed so many times, I still struggle to get past my nerves and enjoy my peace to the fullest... until today :)

I have never played with so much focus and joy as I did today, and I hope that Adam heard me and danced with me while I played, because Adam inspired me to be unafraid to be joyful under pressure.

I was told that he was so filled with God, living everyday with humility and love, that sometimes he wasn't noticed. That showed me that you don't have to be super loud about doing the right thing, because then it becomes about you. When one truly lives in Christ, Christ lives in them, so they become an instrument of his love.

For some reason I found a connection with music, because music isn't about the glory of the piano player, but about the beauty of the peace that the composer wished to convey to the audience.

I can imagine how Adam played his music of love to all those around him, and I too want to be like Him.

Grace

Faith?
In the midst of darkness
I can't even see out of?

Hope?
As my world crumbles
and sifts through my fingers?

Love?
As cold energy
engulfs and defends me?

security
health
companionship
my strength
are all tenuous

anxious
lowly
pathetic
abandoned
I am empty

Alone.
Waiting
to be filled
with You
You to replace me.

Angels to Heaven

While we were still in the hospital after he died, having said my final goodbye, I got up, went back and kissed him one last time and walked out. JohnPaul, Amy, and Kirsty were waiting outside his room (he was in a room with a huge heavy door rather than a curtained cubicle, perhaps because of the gravity of it all). There was a marked pause.

Now what? He was dead, it was all done, I didn't know what to do next. A strange experience, it didn't feel right that it should end so simply and abruptly.

"Well I guess that's it. Do we just go?" I asked.

Amy's response, because of what happened after, was the most important thing anyone could have said. We've known each other our whole lives. She knew me well enough to know that my faith was an important part of my everyday life.

"Nomes, what about a priest? Don't you want a priest?" she asked.

"Oh jeez, of course. Oh my God, Amy. Thank God you thought of it." I replied.

"Can we get a priest? Is there one in the hospital?" she asked the doctor. There wasn't. "Maybe we can call the rectory. We can look up the number."

I gave her the number. I knew it by heart because I had worked there in high school, and like Adam, was an avid prank caller my whole life, and still am. Amy got the answering service, but they could not reach the priests. So, no priest would bless Adam. It seemed so cold and could have been devastating to me, and a lifelong regret, but instead it became a cherished opportunity. Perhaps somehow Adam intervened, as now I would have the gift of directing him to his eternal home.

"You know what? I don't need a priest." I would bless Adam.

I went back to him. I think I said the "Our Father" first. Then I started the "Hail Mary."

"*Hail Mary, full of grace, the Lord is with thee. Blessed are you among women, and blessed is the fruit of thy womb, Jesus. Holy Mary, Mother of God, Pray for us, sinners. Now....*" For those reading who don't share my faith, the final words in that prayer are "now, and at the hour of our death" Here it was, real. The gravity of it hit me. I reached over to hold him again. He did not feel dead or cold, or lifeless. His body emanated peace, strength. It was manly, more virile than defunct. I can't help but think it was his gift to me. As I held him lovingly, I experienced a vision:

I am holding him, even though he is grown. I place him into the arms of two strong angels who took him up into the sky through clouds and place him into Mary's arms. She holds him almost like an infant, like the "Pieta," the famous Michelangelo sculpture of the Blessed Mother, holding the body of her own son, Jesus, after his death. I tell her that he's hers to care for now, and implore her to take good care of him. I'm confident she will, so much that, despite realizing I won't see him for a long time, it's okay. And even though his eyes remain closed, I tell him he's safe, and I know it. I feel no sense that he will miss me or be scared. I know perfectly that he is good, so critical for me as his mom.

Turning to strong angels and a "Mom" in Heaven, a powerful eternal friend who could fill in for me as my precious child was pulled from my own loving protection, was definitely more than just an empty religion default. There was a real and powerful comfort in my faith in something bigger than our loss, pain, sapped strength, and powerlessness, and in something bigger than us, bigger than life, and beyond all of this. I have always had that belief. And the fact that I, a mother, in the moment of her child's death, could experience such reassurance, contentment, and peace is a grace beyond measure or imagination. Without that confidence in his safety, his peace, I would not be here. Despair would have swallowed me.

Today so many people have taken a pass on religion. I get it. In my own Catholicism, a focus on sin and fear, rules and prescriptions that are not up to date with culture, and clergy scandals rivaling the worst daytime soap opera melodrama, have fostered disillusionment and disconnection. At best, young people struggle to find relevance, and, at worst, they're insulted by the hypocrisy. They're not buying in.

But there is more underneath all of that. And if you've tuned out, you're missing out on something. I'm blessed with a faith that holds authentic and meaningful space in my life. It's not surface, or an extraneous obligation, or fear driven, or a box I check to cover the bases just in case there's a Heaven. It is a part of me, of who I am, and it was logical that in my most desperate circumstances I would go there. It was, however, unexpected just how much it came through for me. And as I parted and said goodbye to him for the last time, I was blessed in my gratitude and that comforting vision. The image, and the blessing I was able to bestow on him, are the two most important things (outside of each of my living children) that I possess. I cherish nothing more, except the faith that enabled it: life's greatest treasure, available and accessible to all.

Heaven's Welcome

To: Fr. Tom Petrillo
From: Naomi Brickel
Date: December 16, 2017 10:20am
Subject: Thank you

I have sat to write this so many times, but for some reason this note of thanks to you makes it feel so real, and I always stop. Today I will push through.

Anyway, thank you. For everything. It sounds weird, but the day of Adam's funeral was actually the most joyful of my life, as much, maybe more, than his birth. Everything about the mass was amazing and beautiful, including your very personal and thoughtful homily. You are good all the time, but that was one of the best, and how blessed I feel that it was for Adam. I was so proud of him, and all of those kids of every age, religion, and color who were there representing themselves with such dignity. I was so proud of New Rochelle High School, its diversity, and the fact that Adam had embraced it with such passion and energy.

You have told me to write down the signs from Adam, and I have not had the courage or stamina to do so. But I will make the effort here to share the experiences of Adam's presence I had during the funeral. I think I might have shared them with you already, but perhaps if I

131

write them I can print this out and put it in the beautiful memory book that I hope someday to have the courage to read. ...

Fr. Thomas Petrillo, or "Monsignor," as most call him, is one of my dear friends. He and the other two priests from the parish were the first non-family members to arrive at my door the morning after he died, at around 7am. They were regulars in my house over those initial days and during the visitation. The funeral was a powerful and moving celebration of Adam's life, and he has celebrated special masses on Adam's anniversaries and birthdays, effectively using the opportunities to inspire faith and hope in the large crowds of youth, Adam's family and friends, and all who were impacted.

He's been available to me from the first hours, and in the days, months and years after, buying breakfast, taking a walk, sitting at my kitchen table on a Friday Pizza Night, and through text and phone check-ins. Almost two years after the funeral, Doug's illness became too difficult for me to manage at home. Two days after celebrating mass for Adam's birthday, Fr. Thomas, sat with me at a table in the favorite restaurant we share in common.

Earlier that day I had brought Doug to be admitted into a nursing facility, another grief-filled milestone in our lives. When he heard me mention it on Adam's birthday, along with the fact that I would be alone that night with all the kids away, he had insisted on dinner. "We're going to Lusardi's. You can't be alone like that. I absolutely insist. You can't say no to your pastor." We had martinis and I even got a glass of wine after. I slept well that night, despite my sadness. I know that had he not been the pastor of my parish, and played a critical role in facilitating a more meaningful mature faith for me prior, my faith would likely not have provided the key to survival in the hardships life has presented. I can't envision getting to the place of healing and joy I have achieved without his spiritual influence.

Adam enjoyed his funeral and his spirit and joyful presence were clearly in that church. The first evidence is the lights - yes, lights. Lights would take on a theme. That may be why he decided to make it obvious from the beginning.

I didn't see them, but several people separately recounted it. It was a topic of conversation at the reception at the house after. I wonder how many might have noticed it and never said anything; I'm not sure I would have. They were lights dancing on the high ceiling in the church, reflective lights, similar to how diamonds project the sunlight onto a wall or ceiling (Adam loved diamonds). When you see them, you might need to stop and work backwards to figure out where they originate. It might be the sunlight reflected in a watch or ring worn by someone near a window. What made this somewhat inexplicable was that these lights were rollicking on such a high ceiling, a height difficult for reflections to climb to mirroring even the brightest sunlight, but since it was a damp cloudy afternoon, the sun was hidden. No one was able to trace the source or had an explanation, except that perhaps it was his soul reflecting God's glory. Whatever it was, several experienced it.

The other encounters were more personal. My first experience of Adam's presence occurred during the Consecration portion of the mass. As a Catholic, I was raised to believe in the true presence of Christ in the Eucharist, the bread we receive during Holy Communion. Many Catholics do not understand this faith belief, or believe it, instead seeing the bread and wine as a symbol and not the actual Body and Blood of Christ. From before my First Communion in second grade, I have always believed it. When I received Communion, I knew

God was in me. Throughout my life I have prayed to maintain, and for the continual reinforcement of this belief, as well as the necessary awe, respect, and love. Faith is a blessing that enables people to believe in things that sound crazy and could not be real or possible. I have been blessed because I do believe it. In fact, it's what keeps me Catholic despite so many other issues within the institution. It is a gift to have God so concretely inside me.

The Consecration is the part of the Holy Mass where the priest bestows the blessings and this transformation occurs. Frequently, during this part of the mass I try to hold my attention, experience the Holy Spirit coming down and becoming present all around the church, and permeating the bread and wine. At the funeral, though, it occurred without my willing it; I was too distracted to attend to anything. It simply happened, but was more powerful - and Adam was in it all! I saw, or more accurately felt, Adam and Christ swirling above me together, descending. I perceived a joy in Adam I've never witnessed. His happiness was different, and outward, so filled he was bursting. He was almost Irish jig-like, with some aspect of joyful dancing, but not giddy or silly, a real and spilling ebullience. Words are limiting. I have seen Adam happy, but this was beyond anything. And he came and engulfed me, bringing me into the midst of it, as if I was in this whirlwind of he and Christ.

Reflecting afterwards, my first reaction was that it could not have been real. I had made it up or imagined it. Immediately, though, it didn't matter, there was nothing real about it anyway. "Real" was Adam's laugh when he was actually alive. This was somehow more than real. What is "real" anyway, but what our limited human senses detect in our three-dimensional, time constructed experience? This was so much bigger, so much more beautiful ...

Not to Spoil the Ending... but everything is going to be ok

Joy-full!!

Adam Martin Pope John Paul II Brickel

Text from Lilly Sullivan 1/26/18 12:43pm

*Hi Nomes! Today 2 years ago was Adam's
confirmation. I met with a priest here at
Villanova a couple of months ago to talk about
Adam, God, and life. After I told him I was
Adams confirmation sponsor he was thrilled.
He had the idea that I find out the date of the
confirmation and do something Adam would
have liked to celebrate the Day. So this morning
I ubered to the store, bought white lilies, went
to Starbucks, got a cotton candy frappuccino
for the purpose of the celebration, and a black
coffee for myself, to enjoy. I went to "The
Grotto" on campus, it is a statue of Mary. I
placed the lilies down, had a sip of the cotton
candy, poured some out for Chub, and enjoyed
my black coffee. It was a great start to my day.
Just thought I would share with you so you can
celebrate today too.*

In his homily, Fr. Thomas acknowledged Adam's
Confirmation name, *"Pope John Paul II"* not "John Paul," or even

"John Paul II," but "Adam Martin Pope John Paul II Brickel," a mouthful, grand, and so Adam. He offered a quote from that Pope: "And on the far side of every cross we find the newness of life in the Holy Spirit, that new life which will reach its fulfillment in the resurrection. This is our faith. This is our witness before the world."

Our faith is in a God who knows us, loves us, sustains us, and holds us when our hearts are heavy. And he understands our pain because he walked among us with a human heart. As Christians we also believe in something bigger than death, a resurrection into a new "and improved" life. But there is an aspect that gets overlooked and misperceived. "Heaven" is not just pearly gates or a "Candy Land" in the clouds, separated and far away; God is here too, in and around us: the life force of all existence, a loving life force. As Jesus suffered and endured his earthly suffering, He too was accompanied; the veil is thin and He - and we - are not islands.

Through my suffering over Adam's loss, I've learned that there is a treasure greater than gold, or the nicest pair of sneakers - even spankin' white Yeezys. It is way down, below our lowest bottom, deep in the canyons over the cusps of despair - a Light, Hope. Those depths, rock-bottoms, seem to be the place where Divine Love is more easily detected. I'm sure God does not wait for us to suffer; but perhaps when we are at our lowest - with *nothing* left, where *nothing* else matters - we see more clearly because there's *nothing* to distract us. We are able to detect the One thing that actually matters, the One thing that is "Real."

Dear Mrs. Brickel

Adam meant so much more to me than just a friend. Whenever the friend group was split up it was Adam who brought everyone together and told us that we were being stupid. Whenever we were out, and someone was sitting by themselves, it was Adam who came up to you and said get up and come hang with us. Adam never failed to leave a smile on your face with his jokes or funny sayings that he always came up with, making everyone around him cry with laughter. That is what I admired most about Adam - he was never afraid to be himself, he didn't change personalities to fit in with anyone. To me he was the laugh in a quiet room, the one person that I didn't think twice to tell any problems to, and the crazy idea when there was nothing to do. Adam was a brother to me....

Love

Will R.

Adam's Sun Kiss

The procession out of the funeral was wearying, long and slow, back through all of those people, their red weeping faces. My strength waned with each step and each broken expression, as people caught my eye, or tried not to. I wasn't sure how to react, whether to look up and make contact or avoid faces altogether, wanting to smile, acknowledge, thank, and even comfort, but so spent and drained. I felt myself losing energy and the confidence that I could make it all the way to the doors. I leaned on Doug. Even in his illness, his strength held me up; I don't think I could have made it otherwise.

I got to the doors at the back of the church quite weakened. From the top of the stairs, I looked out at the road and at Adam's casket in the driveway below, surrounded by the priests who had presided at his funeral. The hearse was there, menacingly and threateningly ready; and they began to maneuver him in. A horrible gloom overtook me as I watched him being pushed in, swallowed up. This was it; he would now be cremated. Alone. Adam would become nothing, except over. Gone forever. The permanence was intolerable. A cold damp chill moved through me, penetrating every inch of my body. I felt hollow, vacant, raw, like a frigid empty cave, being filled with a darkness and horror blowing through me. I have never felt anything like it before; I hope I never will again. It was the most dreadful feeling I've ever endured.

Suddenly the priests sang. This was unprompted and unusual, my pastor started and the rest joined in. They sang a beautiful song to Mary, the "Salve Regina." Immediately it brought to mind the vision I had experienced in the hospital as I said goodbye to him, the arms of the angels lifting Adam away, into the loving arms of his Mother in Heaven.

At that moment, a single bright piercing ray of sun burst through the grey thick clouds. A friend was standing in the back of the church near me and saw it. She reported later that my body had been shaking uncontrollably. I looked totally depleted, enervated, was grey and weak, and she worried I might collapse. The ray of light hit my face and chest. I stopped shaking as I felt the light pierce my heart, permeating my entire body with a powerful, comforting, loving warmth. It spread all the way down into my fingertips and toes, chasing away the threatening cold. I was replenished with what I can only describe as Love – Adam - in the deepest most intimate connection I have ever experienced. He was everywhere, touching, warming, and bringing comfort to every cell in my body. I cried out, "Oh Adam!" My pastor thought that the impromptu singing might have somehow upset or pained me. But my cry was not in anguish, rather in delight of our complete connection. His presence was so real. He filled me.

Right after, I was certain that for the rest of my life, I would experience his presence whenever I felt the sun. That would be how he'd stay close, in the light, in the warmth of the beautiful sunlight. But that's not what happened.

The sun hit me just a few days later. I stopped to rest my face in it, let it warm and permeate me, and waited, expectant ...

Immediately I knew he was not there. I was sad at first, having hoped maybe he didn't really have to leave me at all. But my disappointment faded over time, as I realized, and he continues to reinforce, that the fact that he is not in the sun always made that single experience more real and special. In that moment, the darkest and most painful, our final tragic separation, he felt totally gone and furthest; and yet, he found his way to me. I became fortified in the hope that he could be here for me, make himself present when it was needed most. He has, in fact, made a practice of showing up in those moments. It always strengthens me.

Dear Naomi and the Brickel family,

Although it's only been just over a year without Adam, he will forever be one of my best friends. When I think of Adam I start to smile because of how much fun we all had together between the relatable conversations or the funny jokes our group would make that only we would know. Without Adam I wouldn't keep pursuing Track because he told me one day, and I will never forget this, with a smile on his face, "Do what you want to do Mike" for that reason I dedicate every race I run to Adam, he is even on my track spikes. The positive vibe I caught from Adam everyday was crazy because usually everyone our age is so negative, but I loved his attitude, he was so optimistic about everything, whether it was school, rap, or just hanging out. Another thing was that his laugh was so contagious that everything he thought was funny was funny to all of us. Lastly, he was the realest kid out of everyone I had met throughout my life as a fifteen-year-old. If he felt something was wrong he would tell you within a minute. Whether it was a girl you were trying to go for, or going somewhere without all of us, he would question everything. He was the greatest thing to happen to me, and the worst thing to lose. I loved Adam and will forever. I just wish I could say that to him one last time. But when I see him again I won't forget. See you soon Adam

Love,

Mike D.

Soulshine

It was March, just about four months after his death. The time that had passed was short enough that it was still not real, but long enough that the pain was regular and pronounced; short enough that it was the only thing I thought about, but long enough that life had gone back to normal for the rest; short enough that his loss was ever-present, but long enough for friends and family to stop dropping in frequently or ask how I'm doing. I felt him fading from the memory of the community surrounding me.

Life was pretty morose in the Brickel home. We were all under the same roof, in varying stages of acute grief. A full house, and each alone; not enough beds, but an empty one that was a curse on our home. Doug had become more disabled, drifting in and out of sleep most of the day. He often forgot, and might ask if Adam was at school or out with friends. He began to fall more frequently; he bickered with Mindy, with whom he had shared such a close bond. It would have been tough if this was all we were experiencing. And it was March. What is joyful or redeeming about March, even in good times?

It was a Saturday morning. It was only 10am and I was already spinning in negativity. I don't recall what triggered me; it simply could have been that someone came down early and my quiet morning was disturbed. I cherished Saturday mornings when everyone slept in. I relished the time alone. I liked to light a fire and enjoy my coffee, or start bacon so that it was there when they all emerged. Something must have instigated it, perhaps beer cans or a messy kitchen, because I was definitely agitated and angry.

I went next door to my mom's house to borrow an egg. She greeted me in her hopeful and pleasant way, and asked if I'd slept well. It was like a match to dynamite. I opened my mouth and it all burst out. I cried. I was at the end of my rope. So much pain, so much responsibility, such a mess. I was so angry at life, at everyone.

"Naomi, I want you to go back over, and when the kids get up tell them that you need help." (I guess it must have been the mess that got me).

"Are you kidding me? If I go back over there I will kill someone. I literally hate them all! I can't take this anymore!" I sobbed.

"Well, then go back over, grab whatever you need for an overnight, don't speak to anyone, and just get in your car and drive to Westhampton. Oh, and take this measuring tape. I will go over in a little while and tell them that I didn't feel like driving out to measure the rugs (she was planning to take a day trip), so I asked you to, and you'll be back tomorrow."

My mom grew up in Brooklyn, and had spent summers with her family renting in Westhampton Beach, NY. As a kid, she loved to ride her bike back and forth each day to the beach, returning home only for lunch, and spending entire days in the ocean. She was a strong swimmer, and still swims at 86 (even in a blue flag which signals a draggy ocean). She still takes pride in the distinct honor of having been asked in her youth to lifeguard at the town beach, something unheard of at that time for a woman, much less the skinny 15-year-old girl she was. My grandfather had eventually purchased a home, on the same property as his uncle's widow, and both of these homes remain in our family. It's a wonderful place of summer gathering where my mom and the siblings assemble with our families, and cousins have enjoyed growing up together, where Adam's younger cousins got to know him more closely, swimming in the ocean, building sand castles, digging holes, and walking to the bakery or to Rite Aid for candy.

Even in March it would be better than being home. I went back to the house, quietly grabbed flannel pants, a big sweatshirt, a bottle of tequila and limes, and a few other things to make this a relaxing stay. I jumped in the car and started to pull out, but then ran back in for Alexa (the device, not a dog, child, or friend), and grabbed a few logs for the fireplace. Finally, I left and arrived in Westhampton in the early afternoon. I did a few things, like drive down to look at the ocean, run to the store for cheese and candy (the perfect dinner when I'm alone), measure the rugs and report back to Kitty, and put soft flannel sheets on the upstairs bed. Then I lit the fire.

If you happen to be reading this book with your middle schooler, or if you are a niece, nephew, a neighborhood child who looks up to me, or you happen to be Adam's little brother Jude, consider skipping the rest of this chapter. Don't interpret what is to follow as an affirmation of the behavior. Remember, my child had died. That is a really big deal. I was in a very bad place and Adam needed to find me where I was at, in whatever way he could. I don't condone alcohol, any other substances, or cursing outbursts as coping mechanisms. I'm fine if you think to yourself, "She made it up; she had too much to drink." (I didn't; I forget things when I'm overserved.) Like the vision at his funeral, it doesn't matter to me whether anyone discounts it. I could never. I remember and revel in every detail.

I poured myself a drink and tried to relax. Sitting by the fire with my glass, I breathed, became present, and began to cry. I let the tears come. I knew they had been bottled up and needed to come out. I didn't think much, I just let them flow.

I'd been texting my friend Beth, who was out there that weekend too. She'd noticed from our texts that I was down and was worried. She is a nurturer, and without kids of her own to distract, had the space to worry about me. I had stopped responding to texts, so she came to check on me. She's a close enough friend that she can walk into the house unannounced (I have a lot of those), and she did. I was in the bathroom and hadn't noticed the car pull in, and when I walked out she was there. She got a beer and sat by the fire with me (asking questions assessing my mental status much of the time). She did not want me to be there alone in my pain, and tried to get me to join friends for dinner. I had no wish to be out with people, especially those I wasn't close to. I generally didn't after Adam died. So she left.

Her departure left me alone in a way I had not felt before she arrived. Perhaps it was the light that had changed. It was darker. I fell into a deep solitary sadness. I got up for another drink, and went back to the fire. Totally alone. I began to sob.

Forcefully. I screamed up at God, punching the air, yelling loudly, totally unrestricted by the presence of anyone else. I let out my anger as I hit myself screaming.

"F--- you! You can't hurt me anymore. I can do it myself." I kept slapping myself and saying,

"See? You can F---ing move on to someone else. I got this. I'm all set." I've never directed this amount of "Eff you's" at any person. No one but a loving patient God would put up with such an out of control rage. So, I continued yelling, sobbing, screaming, cursing.

I directed it to Adam too. "How dare you tell me to be F---ing happy! You stupid arrogant dick! F--- you!"

I'm somewhat abashed, sharing the horrible language and poison that came out of me. But it did. It was a completely uncontrolled, impassioned rampage. It had to be.

Eventually I got tired and calmer. I let myself cry quietly as I sat there by the fireplace. It was now dark, except for the fire that mesmerized and held my eyes. I still felt so incredibly solitary, as if I had no human connection whatsoever. I longed to be held, comforted, like a defenseless child in safe arms. I knew that was not possible for me, and succumbed to despair. It could not have been worse.

"Alexa, put on psychedelic music."

I proceeded to get lost in the pot-inspired music of the '70s. The Dead, Pink Floyd, Jefferson Airplane, Stones, Beatles, Doors, etc. I let go of my inhibitions, immersed myself in it and made myself present. I heard notes and felt lyrics and their meanings in ways I would typically miss. I played air instruments, drums, guitar, and got deep into the music. Adam was present in the songs. I would see his face and hair, hear his voice, feel a connection between the lyrics and his life and death experiences. I was in it.

An Allman Brothers song came on, "Soulshine." From the first notes I knew it was from him. By the time it finished, I was in tears, and beginning to absorb and process the earliest understanding of his big message for me. It would forever be our song, the connections with the ways he had been present to me resonated in the words, and the meanings were so powerful. Almost as if a song written decades before had been created solely for Adam to use to inspire my healing, it acknowledged my defeated weariness over the last months, the grey day of his funeral, the darkness that had overtaken our home represented through an empty cold hearth, similar to ours the night of his death. The lyrics captured the experience of the cold damp breeze that had permeated my body at the funeral, and communicated the emptiness in the hole left by Adam's loss ... and they challenged me to find my strength - and Adam - right within my own soul. ... Not only in the sunshine ...*Yes, Mom. I was in the sun at the funeral. But I'm here now, always.* Or in the moonshine ... *not in the alcohol.* Or, much less, the rain ... *Yes, mom. Even that horrible rainy funeral day, and I was with you ... I'm always here. Right within your soul. Let it shine!*

Let your Soul shine, Mom!
I'm here.
The spark of Divine within you.
Swirling with Christ.
I Am.
You Are.
All of us within and part of it all,
I'm here, Mom.
I Am!
Let it live inside you.
Let your Soul Shine!

The resonating guitar, Adam strumming, his emotional face. All for me. No mom of a teenager gets this kind of love. The message remained even as other songs came on. Even the intoxication of the emotion and alcohol did not cloud a detail. I was fully present and so was he. I felt warmth and contentment. I danced. He twirled me. I stayed conscious and would not let myself forget. As I continued to enjoy the music, I recorded it all in my mind and haven't forgotten any of it.

A Doors song came on. Adam had the mic and was singing Jim Morrison. He was loving it, and had the best sultry expressions. From Heaven's dimension my brother, Brian, was jamming the guitar, my dad rocking the piano ...

Dad and a piano were cacophony while he was alive. As he had prepared for retirement, he had decided he would take up piano lessons. Honestly, it was fortunate, in just this narrow regard, that he died before he retired. The limited time he was able to devote to piano while he was still working was unbearable.

For my dad, "practice" entailed banging each key individually to deliver its corresponding note. There was no flow, just a slow deliberate, bong ... bong ... bong. He would process the eye ... to brain ... to hand commands; individual clanging notes struggling to reach one another in a flowing tune, each its own individual long, slow, and separate journey ... Now Dad was banging out "Break on Through" accompanying his son and grandson, all three enraptured, rocking it. Adam went from looking into my eyes, to waving the mic in huge arm circles, laughing, singing at and with them, flipping his hair and jumping around the place. It was awesome. I was happy with them, all together. I loved it.

I had poured a drink at 3pm, 5pm, and 7pm (I tend to be precise and 'type A' even in rebellion), a long time to be drinking alone. Lest you judge, remember I had the company of Beth for the first hour, and I was actually never too alone after. If you count the argument with God, partying with Adam, and my brother and Dad cameos, it could technically squeeze in under appropriate, even healthy 'social drinking' norms.

Now it was 9pm. Time for another round, or time for bed. I decided it had been a gift of a night, and chose neither. Instead I'd finish out the song playing, and then just enjoy one more. I waited and watched the fire dying. The last song came on, a repeat. Alexa tends to be good about that in the same sitting. In this case, though, it was being orchestrated by someone even more powerful than Amazon, a kid who always liked to get his way. I'm very sure Adam chose the last song, just to reinforce his presence and message.

"*Soulshine*" played again.

And this time I laughed as I wept, knowing he was there, and had, yet again, made his way to me in my lowest moment.

#CWG

11/12/17 CWG 🩶

~Avery T. - Poonerave   ~RicetooNice   ~DBOMB - Devon B.

~TrillWill - Will O   ~PoonerMike - Mike D.

~Tristan Marine – Poonertime   ~Tommy Pace

~Peter Tomei - PoonerPete ~Tommy Fullerton - Sid the Sloth

CWG will always love you. Forever you're family to every single one of us, you always wanted to be together with NO BEEF just the boys having an amazing time. Your in all of our hearts to the day we die. This isn't goodbye, this is see you soon brotha. We love you. Rest easy. 🩶

... So, what's CWG???

The Sunset Crew

Adam, For the Love of God, what is CWG? I'm going to miss
walking into the house and finding you glued to the computer
playing Minecraft. Even though Kit and I had to yell at you for
following us around all day, you never failed to put a smile on our
faces. … You impacted so many lives for the better and left this world
a little bit better from when you came. So kick back, put your Yeezys
on the desk and watch over your family. I'll miss you, ~Jamie B.

We were not home from the hospital for a half-hour after
he died, before love began to wrap itself around my family and
our home. I can't imagine hope, the most critical piece in my
survival, ever finding its way to the surface in the absence of so
much love.

Weeks later, a neighbor shared that by the middle of that
first morning, he knew all of New Rochelle High School had
heard, and that from above it would have looked like a
procession of ants along the mile-and-a-half walk from the
school to our house. As the hours passed more and more kids
gathered, mostly outside in our yard and driveway, surrounding
Adam's siblings, our basketball hoop, and one another in their
shock. It would be that way through the week, at least until the
funeral. It not only provided me relief knowing my kids were

encompassed by friends, but also the space I needed to begin arranging details and coming to terms (or whatever one calls the state of those first few weeks) with our tragedy.

But it wasn't just the kids from the high school. It started before the next morning and was immediate. There was my mom, my brother Paul, and niece Dana, who spent those first hours numb with us, and JohnPaul's friends, Kevin and Max, who got there within minutes of our arrival home.

For some reason the experience for Kevin's mom, Jen, woken in the middle of the night by her child with such devastating news is one I often imagine and get emotional over. I can hear her voice saying "Oh my God! No Kevin. There's no way. Kevin, stop! Adam Brickel, Oh my God Kevin!" How confusing it must have been, just woken, wondering "what the f---!" To even know what to do when he insisted on being driven over. I have wondered if she felt anxious or concerned that he would be intruding. What's normal when your teenage son's best friend's little brother is suddenly shockingly dead? It took courage for her to bring him to our door, and to just look in. As a mom, my body somehow manufactured protective mechanisms that have numbed me to the trauma of that night, and I feel no emotion when I relive all of the details myself, but get overwhelmed when I imagine the experience of others, like Avery and Ann as they heard on the drive to school, and Kevin's mom, Jen. I'm crying now as I write.

The boys came in quietly, went to their traumatized friend in his room, arranged blankets and pillows on the floor and spent the night there surrounding him. It seemed a simple but strong instinct to crowd in so close. I recall the next morning opening the door, seeing each one curled up in his own blanket, like loyal, protective dogs around the object of their love, as close as they could be. Beautiful and seemingly innate, as they were too young to have experience in something like this. Early the next morning Max's mom, Andrea, came with Dunkin Donuts and sweet coffee drinks for them all. This was the very first example of what would keep surprising me - when responsibilities I was used to would just be taken care of without mention. All of these everyday weights, like feeding kids who slept over, were lifted so I could deal with the real stuff.

Remember the broken thermostat, the missing throw blankets, and the firewood that was lacking on that long cold night as we sat there with no idea what to do? Firewood became something for me to obsess over rather than the trauma at hand. Knowing we would all be close to home for the next several days, like a mom, I began to make lists of things to be done; and the fire became a priority. Kit secured our warmth through the kindness of another friend. Before the sun came up, Jamie Burrell, a lifelong pal to my two oldest, Billy and Kit, was at our door with a wheelbarrow full of wood that he stacked and began to stoke into comforting warmth. Somehow the fireplace stayed lit for a whole week, thanks to ongoing efforts of Jamie and others who just showed up with their wheelbarrows.

My iPhone began to ding and ring before the sun came up. I did not have the capacity for communicating, so I left it in my room. My kids, friends and siblings became operators and receptionists, filtering and facilitating outreach, contacting the superintendent of schools, reaching out to close friends and relatives, taking all of the weight of responsibility to announce or liaise off of me. The parish priests arrived, friends and neighbors assembled, respectfully distanced, to support and help. Some organized food donations, others cleanup, walking the dog, activities to keep Adam's little brother, Jude, 11, busy and surrounded by friends. People I wouldn't have expected briefly appeared in my doorway. Sometimes they would blow a kiss, so as not to crowd, but to ensure we felt their love. The food came fast, furious, and with what seemed an assumption that thousands would need to be fed.

"It has to stop. Seriously, what am I going to do with all of this?" I stressed.

I have this habit of never throwing away food. I love to cook and have always enjoyed the challenge of creatively remaking leftovers. It is almost a compulsion. So, seeing the food accumulating began to feel like a "to do" list. How would I ever wrap it all up? I would be too busy to use up the leftovers. I wasn't in the mood and knew it would be a long time before I felt creative enough to cook. It's interesting how things that were really not important took up space in my head, filled my stress tank - how accumulating food became oppressive.

"I'll tell everyone they need to coordinate through me," Nancy, my close friend since childhood, offered.

"We will make an announcement that people are not to bring food to the visitation." My sister, Mary Gail, added. I did not consider the distress this would cause among my Jewish friends. I remember a work colleague complaining, "We don't know what to do when you tell us we can't bring food! This is what Jews do!" Eventually the food did begin to appear again, but through a more organized and gradual distribution coordinated by my niece, Dana. I had cups, plates, and cutlery for well over a year after.

In all of the organization and activity, there was a particular group of special ladies who became my lifeline. They showed up, a lot, and for months after, never asked (my Irishness would not have permitted it). Regulars, quietly and unassumingly making my life function, grabbing me back on to the end of my rope, showing up to cook for my family with tequila and citrus for me. Nancy even found an authentic old-fashioned citrus squeezer. These friends would stay long enough to distract us from ourselves, living and grieving under the same roof. They had a text thread through which they communicated updates, plans, and strategies for my well-being and our family's survival, "The Sunset Crew." It was a fitting name, as they always showed up in the moments of imposing darkness.

I get teased sometimes for referring to so many as "like my best friend." I have a lot, inclusive of family members. Some are lifelong, some several years, and others more recent. What most share in common is authenticity and an easy laugh. Those closest tend to enjoy a cocktail, prank phone calls, and out of the norm fun. Though Adam's death did not lend itself to lightheartedness, we still found ourselves reaching there often to get through a moment. It inspired deeper loyalty and dedication. I had special people who were "on call," assuming the role of taking weight off, reassigning responsibilities, directing people towards or away from me, nurturing, and in those first few weeks after the funeral, monitoring my progress, keeping tabs, taking turns showing up at cocktail hour, and so on.

Nancy took on the role of coordinator. We grew up a few blocks from each other and had been known as 'Frick and Frack' since elementary school. She has never forgotten a detail or person in our lives - though she conveniently forgets the slumber party I did not get invited to in 3rd or fourth grade. Our relationship has been relatively smooth almost ever since.

One of my first determined accomplishments in childhood, besides learning to ride a unicycle, was riding my bike 'no handed' all the way from my driveway to Nancy's front door. I would get on my bike in the garage and ride out those first few feet using my hands, considering that initial step an acceptable aspect of the challenge. But as soon as I hit the driveway, I removed my hands from the handle bars, steering around and out of my driveway with only my weight and balance. Where the driveway hit the road, I kept the pace slow enough to enable time to view the street, ensuring it was free of oncoming cars, before crossing the sidewalk into the road. This was important, since my brother had been hit by a car outside our driveway right before I was born. He ended up okay, but I always remembered it and proceeded cautiously there. (The way caution dissipated within ten feet was obviously a shortcoming of young age.) Once I hit the road, faced with an immediate uphill, I had to pump the pedals vigorously up through the first right turn, posing little risk or danger. After that, however, success necessitated no brakes and ignoring four stop signs (one at a pretty busy intersection and the final posing the most critical step to success). If I slowed down even slightly as I went down the short hill and across the five-way intersection into her driveway, I would never be able to make it up the gravel driveway to the front door. Even under the most conducive circumstances - no cars - this last part posed the greatest challenge, and more often than not, a final frustration and end in failure. It was a rare but highly celebrated success when I did it. As I look back now and consider the trickle down over generations that just one quick interaction with a car would have generated, I am thankful and fortunate that the potential implications of my stupidity were not realized. Nancy and I have certainly grown into much better adults than anyone could have hoped for.

She was there early that first morning accompanied by the gradually forming cadre she would organize into the group "Sunset Crew" text. These friends showed up, held me up, and were critical, lifesaving support over the next two years. She was such a close friend that she accompanied me to the funeral home. Her sister Irish designed and printed the funeral program. The support and generosity from the community and so many friends and neighbors would filter through her communication and organization. People would volunteer their kindness and check on my well-being through her. For the first year, she became part of most of the important moments, holidays, and frankly, most cocktail hours. She was also the one that would begin to drag me back out and accompany me, as I slowly returned to social engagement after a few years.

From those first hours that morning after his death, I was plagued by anxiety and hyper-focused on a strange but threatening reality - the fact that eventually I would need to go to bed, alone to confront my new life, the one without Adam, and face the torment of his loss. I vividly recall the light in my kitchen at different times during that first day, present with that strange thought haunting me. I don't recall whether I shared it, or spoke of it out loud, but it was somehow evident enough for my friend Beth - the same Beth who'd shown up that Soulshine afternoon - to notice.

Beth and I grew up in the same town and became friends in high school. She was a tall, athletic senior when I was a freshman, and popular, pretty, and friendly. She is a natural athlete, and being one myself, I looked up to her for her inspiring innate talent. The thing that stood out most about Beth in high school, though, was her kindness. She would drive me home from practice and treat me like an equal, even as a JV underclassman. I was always grateful and nervous in the back seat, but she never leveraged her seniority. I don't think it was in her to feel it. Though we saw each other through mutual friends over the years, our friendship had been diverted by our different lives and my own preoccupation raising a big family. We reconnected at the beach about five years before Adam died.

She has not changed much. When I think of Beth now, still the first words that come to mind are gentle, humble, pretty, funny, kind. She was away when Adam died and called me as soon as she heard. Hers was one of the first messages I listened to hours or days later, and I still remember the pain in her voice and how it shocked me from my own numbness. She was a fixture in my kitchen within hours of returning from her trip. While I only vaguely remember details of her presence that day, I will never forget what happened that evening.

As people cleared out and the first day wrapped up, she didn't. She lives in NYC, but was going to stay nearby with her parents in her old family home. My kids and their friends were hanging out in the kitchen, and I was suddenly overcome with exhaustion. Despite my fear of being alone, I was ready for bed.

My youngest, Jude, was unable to sleep in the bed, room, or house, where 24 hours earlier he had experienced the worst trauma of his short life, and went over to sleep with his "God-family," the Sullies. He would sleep there for the next six weeks. And I moved into Adam's bottom bunk, where I slept for the next nine months. When Jude did finally come back to sleep at home, I was there in the bed under him. He would never have been able to acclimate to being alone there.

I started upstairs to confront my horrific new reality. This was the moment I feared. With the noise of people behind me, this grave moment was like walking through a thick heavy metal door slamming loudly behind me. I was faced with the realization that what was on the other side is not only locked away forever, but has also crumbled and disintegrated into nothing, dust. The last time I slept I had fallen off as the mom of a complete family. Now I had a new identity, though I was still unaware how defining it would become. Of course, I could never be the same. But going forward people would also see and treat me differently, thinking "that poor woman,"' wearing new expressions when they met me, even looking away to avoid, too pained to engage. I walked slowly upstairs towards the bleak forever.

And Beth was behind me.

"I know where to go." I kidded.

"I'm just gonna come with you. Pull up the sheets," was her light response. Beth keeps a neat house, Adam and Jude didn't.

On the way up, JohnPaul asked her to wait so he could talk to me in private. He needed a few minutes to let me know he was ok, and would be ok. I was glad we had that chance to be alone together and check in. It was nearly 24 hours since he had woken me with the now answered question, "Where's Adam?" I encouraged him to not stay up much longer, knowing we would have long days ahead. As he left he sent Beth back up.

I changed and got myself ready. When I came out Beth had straightened the bed, gotten me water, plugged in my phone, and put a wooden chair next to the bed. I had built Adam's bottom bunk, and it was raised higher than normal. I thought when I built it that it would be fun to get up into, and hoped the boys would keep their clothes in drawers underneath. I've always tried to be creative, finding innovative and inviting ways to entice the kids to use anything other than the floor as a wardrobe. Adam had hung bedsheets around the bottom to create a "cave" for Kelly to sleep in. Something prompted me to pull them aside to look in. I discovered all of the missing throw blankets that I had assumed Doug misplaced. Adam had taken every single one to create a cozy and elaborate dog bed for Kelly. I laughed. I was happy Beth was there to experience this last piece of him, that I was not alone when I found it, and had someone to smile with me. She stood by out of the way while I climbed up and got under Adam's sheets. Once I was settled she sat down in the black chair.

"I can't believe it's here. I am exhausted so I guess I'll be fine, but I've been so afraid of this moment."

"I know. I'm going to stay until you're asleep so you don't have to worry. What time is church tomorrow? I know you want to go. I will pick you up and take you. I mean, if you want me to. I mean do you want me to?"

"Yes. If you don't mind I'd appreciate that. Thank you." I practically snored...

Beth is married to a woman. Though she was brought up Catholic, her religion has not been a part of her adult life. That is the case for many kids I grew up with, disproportionally for those who are gay. Even with the more inclusive pastoral leadership of our current Pope Francis, and despite Christ's inclusive outreach and messages and themes within our Gospels that focused on love, inclusivity, mercy and non-judgement, our church is just not a welcoming spiritual home for gay people. For most, Beth included, it has been easier to just leave. Now, here she was offering to bring me to 6:45 a.m. mass on a Tuesday morning. So much more Christ-like (when you actually stop to think about it) than how our church decides whose welcome at the liturgy table...

I fell asleep quickly. I don't even recall if we spoke about anything, but I wasn't alone. The immense threat that had loomed over me the whole day, through Beth's simple but profound act of kindness, was nothing. I fell asleep with her sitting there and the next morning she was outside my front door waiting at 6:30 a.m. to take me to church. I was able to bring it all to God, where I always went in low moments and fear. I didn't worry about being alone, or if someone would recognize me and approach, or about feeling eyes burning into me. I was wrapped in the protection of my friend and her conscious deliberate charity.

So, Jamie Burrell, "For the love of God, what is CWG?"

Well, I never really got the exact story, but it's an acronym a group of boys gave themselves in middle school. I've been assured by an insider I trust, that it's not inappropriate, drug-related, sexual, racially offensive, chauvinistic, or demeaning to anyone - just a dumb name made up by a bunch of dumb middle school boys. Yet, it's quite clear to me now, three years after first hearing it, that it represents much more, embodying clear values for the young people who use it: brotherhood, friendship, family, watching out for each other, excluding no one, "NO BEEF," and no "Fake."

And, Jamie, I think it's something else, too. It's what is underneath and what drives the behavior of getting out of bed in the dark, going outside to the back of your property, loading up a wheelbarrow with firewood, and walking it the half mile at dawn to the house of your lifelong friends, just so they won't be so darn cold as they absorb the shock and grieve the sudden death of their little brother, the one you loved and who made you laugh. Thank you, Jamie.

And thank you Beth, and JohnPaul, and Nancy, and Mary Gail, and Hope, and the Sullies, and.... and... and...

Funeral Friends

I knew little of Adam's life before he died besides the facts that he teased his siblings, baked cookies every day, was a picky eater, played Minecraft very well and often, and got exasperated with me when I double checked about walking the dog and doing homework (since I was usually asleep before he did either). His Minecraft addiction lessened somewhat in the months before he died, but had caused me concern about potential issues with friends, or lack of them. A needless worry, I was so wrong.

And he definitely enjoyed his funeral. It would be impossible not to when he had the lead role in such an incredible tribute to a life. It was packed, with over 1000 people. Those who could not fit spilled down the long church steps all the way to the road and across the street. Throngs for Adam, for our family, and so much palpable love in one place. It was hard not to be joyful, as we had come to learn, Adam preferred. I do not recall a sad energy, though I am sure there were many sad people there. We walked into the packed church. My heart beats fast as I remember all the people, and feeling intimidated by all the eyes on us. So many focused on our tragedy, our pain. I actually noticed just a few faces, some smiled, others had tears, many I recognized but couldn't think of their names (this unsettled me), many I did not even know.

I saw my friend Pat, and I can still recall the great comfort I felt seeing her there. Hers is one of the only faces I remember in the crowd. Pat has been very important to me these last years. She, too, lost a son. We became close a few years after he passed, connected through our work. She was an iconic leader for me professionally, a serious person, and brilliant. I was always humbled by her respect for my opinions and perspective; she lifted me in my career by encouraging my voice and confidence.

She also happens to be a bit intimidating. So, being woken up in the middle of the night in Westhampton one summer, long before Adam died, by a voice in my head suggesting - no demanding - that I give her a book about a near-death experience, knowing she had lost a child, triggered an easy, automatic response from my left brain and professional instinct, "No effing way." The voice had felt real. It had literally woken me, but I didn't care. I ignored it. It felt as crazy as it sounds, and challenged whatever social intuition I possessed to listen. But, it kept weighing on me, and eventually I sent her the book. Our friendship evolved from there, two full years before Adam's death. Weird.

Now she was right there on the aisle, catching my eye and sharing her strength as I processed into my own son's funeral. She had traveled almost three hours to pay respects at my house, and found a place to stay so she could be at the ceremony too. I was told she was the first person in the church; perhaps she needed to ensure she got a seat where she could see and support me. Pat is a gift in my life, a friend who's accompanied me in a way no one else could have. How strange is the way we became connected so long before Adam's death? But then, life is strange and, I've learned, much bigger than our concrete experiences.

It was a relief to walk straight to the front where I would not be facing all of the people present. It would have been distracting to see everyone through the whole mass and ceremony. Instead we were up front surrounded, in many ways protected, by rows of my large and extended family. After we were seated, a group of young people assembled at the church's side door, just to our right. They were a part of the overflow at the main doors and had been redirected this way. As they entered, we could not avoid looking up at and noticing such a diverse group of very large young men. Who were they, and how did they know Adam?

"Mom, that's the football team!!" Jude whisper-screamed. The New Rochelle High School Football team! Adam had spent his last Saturday night upstate, watching them compete in the state semi-final game. Even though they had lost that game, they were heroes.

I didn't understand. Why were they all here? Did they actually know Adam? I have only cried twice while writing these memories, but I'm crying now. The image of these young men, several of whom I'm now close to, walking through the doors, seen by everyone in the church, was a gift for me, for Jude, for JohnPaul, for Doug (a former HS and college football player himself), for all of us - and a tribute to Adam. I was proud that this strong and impressive group of men were here. I was so proud of them, in their dignity, solemnity, and reverence; and for Adam, that they had chosen to be here for him.

I was also gratified by the diversity of those present. I'm sure Adam's funeral rivaled few other occasions for the largest congregation to ever fill and surround our church. I am sure it's diversity – in terms age, color, culture, and even religion - has not been surpassed either.

Who was this boy, my child, to attract so many? And how was it that they all considered him such a close friend?

Dear Naomi,

Adam meant a lot to me and to everyone. But I think you know how kind, funny, and thoughtful he was. So instead of me telling you a story about how much he meant to me, I want to tell you a story from when we were little, that really shows how much he cared for his friends, and especially you.

Me and Adam were in third grade and we were sitting on the trampoline relatively late at night. We were talking about all kinds of stuff like the girls we like and normal third grade stuff. Adam suddenly asked me what I thought happened to people when they died. I told him I hope we were reborn into new lives because to me it seemed like the most logical thing. Adam then told me that he hopes we are not reborn when we die. I asked him why, and he said that he didn't even want to imagine living in a new life, in a different neighborhood, with different friends, with a different family, and he especially couldn't imagine living with a different mom.

I know because we were in third grade the story seems like a stretch, but I promise you it is true. Knowing how content Adam was with his life consoled me during the toughest times this past year, and I thought you should know the story, and just how much Adam loved you.

Tommy P.

Touching my Hand

I had my first Adam dream about 6 weeks after he died. It is really the only dream I've had where he is fully present. I have since had a night where I was awakened by his voice, and another dream related to him with a purposeful message. But this was the only one where he was very clearly "here," and I fully remember it. I hope it's not the last.

I was sleeping in his bed. Being in the place he spent eight hours every night made me feel closer to him. It took me a while to change the sheets, longer than I would typically let go between bed changes. It was hard to let go of any remaining traces of him, including his slept-in sheets. Another special spot is the desk in the living room where he played Minecraft for so many hours of his life. It was months before I could move his laptop from the place he last played it. Eventually I took over that spot too, and I have written most of this narrative right there. There is also a blanket and certain spot on the living room couch that I like to be in for the same reasons.

This dream was vivid. We were on a family vacation at a beach house, unfamiliar and no place I have ever been. I was in a nook off the kitchen, heating something in a microwave. There was an open, screened window next to me. As I was waiting, Adam was suddenly standing right outside the window. I could see him from his chest up. His dark hair was the same as it always was, with a part hanging down in the front that he often flipped back with his hand. I knew he was dead, but he was there and spoke to me. His voice was crystal clear. I continued to remember it for a while, though I had experienced difficulty recalling his voice the weeks prior. His presence was so real and his words so natural that I actually began to think he was back, and that somehow he was really there on vacation with us. I finally said to him, "So, are you going to come to the beach with everyone?"

"I can't. I'm the dead one. Remember?" He gently responded, smiling humbly, almost apologetically, as he began to move away.

"Wait! Adam! Wait. You have to at least touch me!" I put my right hand up to the screen, the thin veil separating us. He shook his head to say he couldn't, shrugging his shoulders as if to say it wasn't something he could change.

"Adam! No! Come back here. You have to touch me! You have to!" I demanded. I was, I guess, what Adam and Johnny would call, "needing to chill."

He looked at me, shook his head in exasperation, in his "jeez, why you so tight?" way, and reached up with his index finger to touch the palm of my hand. The screen separated our flesh, but the pressure still penetrated and I felt him against me. Then he was gone, and I woke up.

I lay in bed in the middle of the night with the vivid details of this dream still present. I was so happy and filled. I remembered every word he said. I remembered his voice, hair, and expressions so clearly. I knew I should get up and write it all down; I willed myself to get out of bed, but I fell back to sleep. When I woke the next morning, he was still clear and present. I could still hear his voice. But his words were gone. I worked to remember and bring it back, but I couldn't. His touch, though, remained. I felt it still. The center of my palm is sensitive. It is a place on my body, where, if touched lovingly, sends a connection miles into me to a place deep and intimate. His touch reached me there. His words are gone, but his love remains. He was reluctant to touch me. But in the end, when he saw I needed it, he came through for his mom, as a son should, even if she's "ackin all crazy."

And I'll always treasure it.

Halloween

In the version of grief we imagine, the model will be
"healing." A certain forward movement will prevail. The
worst days will be the earliest days. We imagine that the
moment to most severely test us will be the funeral, after
which this hypothetical healing will take place. ... We
have no way of knowing that the funeral itself will be
anodyne, a kind of narcotic regression in which we are
wrapped in the care of others and the gravity and
meaning of the occasion. Nor can we know ahead of the
fact (and here lies the heart of the difference between grief
as we imagine it and grief as it is) the unending absence
that follows, the void, the very opposite of meaning, the
relentless succession of moments during which we will
confront the experience of meaningless itself.

Joan Didion, *The Year of Magical Thinking*

There is so much I have blocked out from the first year.
I was numb for much of it, though not completely. It was a dance
between the devastation and trauma, and a threatening
awareness that I was not fully processing his death. Unnerving.
I knew it was worse, and would come in time, like a reckoning.
This is a narrative focusing on lights within the darkness, but it's

important to note it was an evolving process. It would be silly, "fake," to suggest that the first year was anything but hell, with some bright spots that felt few and far between.

There was an issue that plagued me, and only got worse as time passed. Adam's loss was my only 'real' reality, pervasive and always there. It was the first thing I thought of when I awoke, and what I fell off to sleep with. It wasn't always all-consuming or heart wrenching, but I was never without it. As time passed, it didn't lessen for me, but I began to perceive it getting better for others. There were exceptions, people who came to my door with gifts, in tears. I stopped going to the grocery store and let Amazon bring it all to me. This way I could avoid stares, people looking down so as not to make eye contact, or being hugged by someone crying with comments, like, "I couldn't bring myself to reach out but ... ." For the most part, though, people were kind, and likely just not sure how to act. Eventually they stopped reaching out, asking how I was, or talking about him at all. Perhaps they didn't want to upset or trigger me. Outwardly I projected strength, and maybe others didn't want to be responsible for upsetting it. Even in my own family, even with my own kids, because all of us were all processing our grief differently, we did not share our pain and loss together. We were too raw and exhausted. So, it hounded me that I was plagued by this primal reality, but others were healing and moving on. Being practical, I rationalized, knowing how it worked. I have lost loved ones. You heal. Life goes on and their memories fade. It was happening around me, but that could never happen for me. I thought he was being forgotten and felt very alone, and, quite frankly, broken.

I was blessed to find the right person to work with as I processed my grief. This was important. Without someone really effective, outside of me, so much truth would have been distorted in the harsh cruelty I leveraged on myself. Some are prone to an accompanying self-disdain when suffering. Although I have done a lot of work in these past years to get over it, it was definitely in my repertoire. I scorned my own vulnerability, sensitivity, and emotion, even though in my work and friendships, they are the very qualities that make me successful and connected. My willingness to put myself out there and share my experiences raising a child with disabilities with truth, feeling, and emotion, has enabled me to be more impactful, empathetic, and helpful to other families, and to inspire professionals to feel empathy and passion in their day to day work. These same traits engender the authentic deep, friendships I enjoy. And yet, it's these aspects of my personality - prized for making me better in my work and in my personal relationships - I scoffed at and disparaged as weakness around my tragedy.

Prior to Adam's death I worked with a therapist off and on for some years. In my initial shock, I had no desire to go back. I was frightened by my lack of feeling, and not ready to engage in a therapeutic process in those first months for fear of what it might trigger. I felt threatened by what I had yet to face. When I did finally make an appointment, it didn't work. My therapist had experienced his own horrible tragedy that I learned of just a few months before Adam's death. Now, knowing what we shared in common, I found myself stumbling as I shared my experience, fearing I might trigger his and comparing. A therapeutic relationship was no longer a fit, and perhaps therapy was not something I would need for this anyway. I could "lean in" as the self-help books suggested, and rest in my strong faith.

Of course, no human foundation, no matter how strong or solid, is meant to withstand the death of a child. Moms were simply not engineered that way. Unaware, I began to sink into a quicksand of desperation and fear. My kids were struggling simultaneously. We were all in different places, on top of each other, with no room to process our grief, yet needing to. I remember one afternoon when the house was empty, and I decided to lie down on the couch in Adam's old spot, and just cry. With no one around, no kids who would worry seeing my sadness, no one to take care of, I could settle into my sorrow, and let my tears flow. I lay there and let myself feel sorry for me. Then the deck door opened. It was Johnny.

"Mom! Mom?" he yelled.

"I'm right here, Honey," I popped up off the couch.

"What are you doing??" he asked, trying to determine if he should be worried.

"Nothing, nothing. I just had a few minutes to lie down. I'm so tired for some reason, and just decided to close my eyes for a few minutes. I'm fine. I promise."

I hid my tear-stained eyes, juggling my dual roles of broken *and* worried mom. It's unfortunate but obvious that when families suffer loss or pain, that first role is inevitably accompanied by the latter. The death of a child impacts every person in the family - each so deeply and individually. At the same time, of course, the levels of stress in the care and worry for the other children are compounded.

Things were clearly not going well. Our home and lives, individually and collectively, were crumbling. I started to get a lot of advice.

"They should be helping you more."

"Maybe you could set up a schedule where everyone cooks one night."

"How about some rules or expectations for when they come home?"

"Someone needs to clean up those beer cans outside the house."

"I hate that you're spoken to that way. Maybe you should tell them they need to ..."

Each outreach or well-intentioned advice was a straw that felt like a boulder on top of the rest. I was not sure where to begin, or how much more any of us could handle.

"Of course we are all a mess and our house is a wreck, Adam effing died!!"

Amy, next door, reached out with the name of a therapist friend from the community who had expertise in working with grief. Adam's death impacted our community widely, and even this woman's own family indirectly. She had offered assistance if needed for the kids. Amy had expressed concern for JohnPaul and the trauma of that horrible night. I felt it too, and was worried about all my kids. So I called her friend, Caroline.

Caroline was my lifeline in the tempest. Our first conversation provided solace owing to her ability to understand and normalize. Her advice was doable rather than wishful, as simple as a few contacts to try for the kids. Her help was productive, offering direction rather than observations, and relief, instead of more weight. Just as I was beginning to feel an element of control, ready to hang up and begin the follow up, she asked a simple but penetrating question.

"Are you taking care of yourself? How are you?"

My instinct was to quickly reinforce my battalions.

"Yes. Thanks. I am good. I'm doing what I need to do." Ugh. I felt my strength wane, and I was welling up, the tears were imminent. Her simple question was piercing, like kryptonite. I became keenly aware of how un-okay I was, breaking inside trying to navigate my grief, the lack of feeling, the stress of work, the worry over the kids, the concern about Doug, the anger about Doug, his illness and the resulting emotional and even physical absence, my encompassing solitude and loneliness.

"If you ever want to meet, I'm happy to speak with you."

"Ok. Maybe that would help. Thank you."

We set up a time, and I'm sure Adam coordinated the contact. Caroline was certainly the right person for me in this process. She is not fake, at all, and has the perfect combination of objectivity and moxie to work with someone like me, a sensitive and feeling, yet a protective Irish wall builder. A critical element in my healing and eventual happiness, was something she introduced into my grief process: Truth. She helped redirect energy spent self-loathing my "weakness" into a more appropriate and objective neutrality towards my anguish. She challenged, without offending, when I rationalized behaviors of myself or others. And she had her own unique way of shining light on the facts, bringing in an authentic perspective, rather than simply validating mine to the point of enabling.

Caroline is a special person who crossed my path at the right time. I have ceased believing in all the coincidences, so I express my gratitude to Adam and to God for assisting with the connection. She is another bright star that appeared in the dark night. My happiness today is due in large part to her talents and expertise. I texted her recently with some exciting but unsettling news. Her response back sums up best how we got there:

As our friend Eckhart says...

"Life will give you whatever experience is most helpful for the evolution of your consciousness.
How do you know this is the experience you

need? Because this is the experience you are
having at the moment."

I am happy for you.

Being from the community, Caroline also knew that I was wrong in my perceptions about Adam fading from memory, and that Adam's friends were still mourning him significantly. I did not yet know any of them beyond the quick intros and condolences at the wake and funeral, where I had met hundreds of kids. But she did, and offered concrete examples to show me. I am still so grateful for her efforts and evidence, because even with her authentication, it was something I needed to work through, necessitating time and its accompanying loneliness.

But it was on Halloween, almost a year after his death, that I fully realized my mistake. The impending anniversary, just two weeks away, posed a looming stress associated with my own developed timeline to heal. "It takes a year to grieve," I had somehow naively decided. I was up against the clock. Why was I still so dead inside?

Halloween has always been one of my favorite holidays, mostly because it means unrestricted candy, everyone's fantasy, or at least always mine and my kids. I decided not to make a big pot of soup or invite family to stop in like I did most other years, but I was still looking forward to having kids ring the bell. I would enjoy it with a fire lit, wine, and dinner with my mom and our friend, Eileen, who was visiting from out of town. It was a quiet night with few doorbell rings. Every year it was hit or miss, depending on kids' and parents' comfort levels in the dark on a busy road. It was a quieter year in the house, too, with all of the kids out. Getting past the time for trick or treaters, my mom, Eileen, and I were in the kitchen prepping dinner. Surprisingly, the bell rang.

At the door were three high school girls. The first, Christina, was a neighbor whose parents I knew. I had discovered during the wake and funeral that she and Adam were good friends. I was constantly shocked as I came to learn of Adam's social circle. It was vast but I never knew it. Whenever he would leave the house, and I asked who he was meeting, he always used those same three names, Will, Tommy, Avery... some others were interspersed now and again, but he mostly kept me in the dark. I had no idea while he was alive that he knew any girls at all. It was nice to see Christina, and it was kind and thoughtful that she had come to my door and brought friends, who I figured must also have known him.

"So, were you all friends of Adam's?" I asked.

All three looked at me so intensely, and with so much love (not sure how I quantified this). Their gazes pierced my protected soul. I felt their pain and could see the sadness they had carried the last year. I experienced their love for Adam and love for me in that moment, as the person standing there in front of them most closely connected to their lost beloved friend.

Those beautiful girls shattered my wall. Their eyes looked through me. Their love and vulnerability pierced mine. It took every effort to contain myself and keep it together long enough to give them candy, make them feel appreciated (they were so appreciated) and close the door. And when I did, I could not contain my tears, they erupted from me. I cried and cried. It had taken their piercing, loving, expressive eyes to shatter the wall of protection I had built around my heart, and my misperceptions that I was the last sole mourner. I knew wholeheartedly that I was not alone. Jamie, 'Stina, Ella. I will never forget your loving faces or the healing that began for all of us that day.

The Anniversary

Anniversaries, even with the best therapeutic and family support, are difficult. The weeks leading up to the first imposed a constant threat. It did not help, but was typical of my finish-line approach to most things in life, that somehow I had decided it only takes one year. As the date got closer, I was still so broken and lacked any desire for healing. For me, recovery implied further separation, and I was desperate to hold on. I willed him to remain. I had not yet fully digested "Soulshine Adam:" no longer constrained by time and physical boundaries of matter, but present within and encompassing me. That concept was a light that still needed fuel.

Though I started this narrative right at the moment of the crisis on the street, earlier in the evening the night he died had been memorable in itself. Nancy had asked me to join her to go meet friends, but I had refused the invite, looking forward to a Brickel family night with Chef Kit. The eight of us and my mom, Kitty, enjoyed a special night, special even if what came after had never happened. Billy had recently moved back into the house after a short stay living with a friend, and we were all under the same roof. I recall where I sat at the table, the pride I felt seeing my grown children enjoying each other, and what good looking, kind young adults they were growing into! I now cherish the memory and those images as the last time we would enjoy our whole family together.

Kit, 22, had recently graduated from college and was enjoying the first months of her first "real" job. She had offered, like an adult, to make us a chili dinner. Adam was a picky eater and I remember him standing by the stove next to me, cooking a grilled cheese in my favorite cast iron skillet. (The simple fact that I wrote that last sentence brings a new realization and appreciation that he cooked his last meal in the same pan I use most mornings. This association will make me enjoy it even more. How far I have come when a frying pan is a light that lifts me!)

Kit chided, "Adam, I can't believe you aren't eating my dinner!"

"Shoud'na made chili." he responded in his slang affect, pursed lips, and playful "I told you so" expression.

"Adam! You need to stop talking that way. You are going to get in the habit and insult someone or forget one day," his grandmother, Kitty, half-sternly reprimanded. A playful, normal but memorable, love-filled Sunday family dinner. Undoubtedly, a night I would have remembered even if life had gone on normally, but now it's a precious memory and gift to cherish.

For the first anniversary we would recreate that dinner. The Kirks and Paces - those who had shared the crisis - would join us, along with my siblings and families. We planned a Sunday dinner, the night before the actual date, with chili and grilled cheese. On Adam's anniversary schools were closed for the Veterans' Day holiday. My pastor would say the 9 a.m. mass for Adam.

Adam's friend Peter reached out to see if he and a few others could stop by.

"Yes, of course. That would be such a gift for me. And Peter, I know Adam had a lot of friends who I don't know. Please let them know they are welcome to come by on Sunday, or to the mass on Monday. I'm going to have bagels at the house after. I want everyone who would like to come to feel free to join us for any or all. I would love to get to know everyone better."

Peter's mom, Stephanie, reached out after to be sure I understood the implications of my invitation. She said to expect a full house and offered to help organize. I certainly underestimated the numbers. There must have been 40 or 50 kids, a large and diverse group from different backgrounds, friend groups, interests, and again (it always surprised me), the athletes. Before they left Sunday night I took "stage" on a bench at my kitchen island, thanked all for coming, invited them to the mass the next day (not expecting most would) and I shared a little about Adam.

I pointed out that I was wearing mismatched argyle socks, that I had decided to wear a "pair" of Adam's socks deliberately. In the Brickel home socks are not worn in matched pairs. I am not sure why or how it evolved, perhaps it's a generational thing. I recall a fashion fad where Kit wore unmatching colored ankle socks that she had purposefully switched. This had become permanent in our house. Though I would occasionally spend satisfying time dumping the basket of mismatched, clean socks on the kitchen table and sorting them, most often, socks were just pulled out of the basket without appropriate pairing. It seemed that the boys were actually deliberate about not pulling socks from the same pair, even separating matches. For Adam there was another detail, argyles.

I also told them about the boy in Adam's chemistry class, the one I would speak about in the graduation speech, who Adam had gone to, noticing his sadness, and assured it was going to be ok. That young man had gotten up at a candle service at the high school the following spring to speak about Adam, he had told his story, and finished poignantly with a tear-filled question, "Who's going to tell me it's ok now?" The kids would cherish a memory of Adam. Why not share one that offered an example to imitate. I encouraged them to wear mismatched socks one day in his memory, and to use the visual not only as a reminder of Adam, but of his simple and impactful act of kindness, and to remember to see those that they might otherwise miss. And I invited them all to come to church the next day, for Adam's mass.

The church was as crowded as a scaled back funeral, full of friends and even kids who never knew him. Many parents came too. My sister, Mary Gail, and sister-in-law, Hope organized the bagel breakfast. We were surrounded by the people who had shared that horrible night, as well as the days, weeks, months that followed: my family, the Sunset Crew, neighbors, and perhaps most beautifully, his friends, the people who knew him best, yet we had never known.

The suffering I had experienced thinking he was forgotten, that I was alone in my sorrow, was dispelled. I listened to them recount dreams, and funny stories and antics, laughing and crying over the memories and stories. I could see their desire to be near his family and home, to know us, as if through his family they might somehow reconnect. It was surprising to see a group of teenagers drawn to an adult, me; it was beautiful, inspiring and exhausting, a precious and emotional gift.

I was in the kitchen hours after the mass that morning, the bagels gone, things cleaned and put away, sitting at the table with my mom and sister, running out of steam. The kids were still in our living room, barely trickling out, in Adam's space, around his desk, and the couch where he chilled. As I think back, I wonder if he drew them there.

"I'm fried. I think I'm ready for them to go," I said to my mom.

"Why don't you go in and tell them you have to go out," Kitty replied. "You're exhausted and need some time to rest."

I wanted them to go, but never wanted them to leave. I decided to go in and interject myself. I would regret not connecting once they were gone. It felt a little awkward because none of us knew each other; it almost felt like intruding, even in my living room. As I sat on the couch, I noticed two girls off to the side. I now know it was Lyla and Jamie. Jamie was one of the Halloween girls. She was crying and Lyla was consoling, trying to calm her. Lyla is a mature, acute girl, and seemed to not want me upset by the tears of his friends on this day. I went over to them.

"It's ok to cry here. I cry every day. All these months I thought I was alone; I actually thought he was forgotten, that all of you had moved on, and it was so hard. It's good for me to see I was wrong. I'm sorry for your pain, but it's totally ok to cry in front of me. You can cry here... But here, come here, don't cry, it's ok."

I hugged Jamie, fighting back my own tears. I hugged all the kids. And before they left I asked them to stay close, remain a part of our lives, that my door was always open. One of the girls, Laura, said we would plan a dinner. It sounded great and I agreed, but in the back of my mind assumed it would never happen.

They left, everyone was gone. Except Beth. Beth who stayed with me the first night until I slept, who came back to take me to early mass, who showed up in Westhampton when I was sad and alone. Here she was again in a similar role. She stoked up the fire and sat on the couch. My kids had gone off with friends, and Doug was watching sports upstairs. Exhaustion and sadness simultaneously overtook me. I lost energy to talk. She left, reluctant to leave me alone, but needing to be back in the city and knowing I needed to rest. As I closed the door behind her, I was overcome by a dark cloud, desolation and isolation. I lay on the couch by the fire, in Adam's regular spot, under the same blanket he liked to cover up with, and cried until I slept.

I woke a few hours later. It was dark and the fire was dying embers. Before I opened my eyes, I became aware of an encompassing gloom, brief seconds lying half asleep, realizing I was waking, threatened by the present, the coming hours, the next day, my entire future. The milestone was here and gone, time to move forward, to leave Adam, all of it, in the past. In that brief half-waking instant, I was conscious of an interminable "rest of my life" without him, the difficulty of my life circumstances, my solitude and my loneliness. I was being woken by despair.

The phone dinged.

It's tommy. I found this on our computer the other day thought u might like it 🖤

Tommy was Adam's playmate and best friend most of their lives. It is strange sometimes to see the man he has grown into, and especially to hear his grown up voice, because when I think of him, I'm taken back to memories of the little boy knocking at my door forcefully, with his shoulders back and chest out, inquiring in his endearing raspy lisp whether Adam was free to play. There are one-liners of Tommy's as a young kid that still make me laugh. I hope to be sharing them after too much wine at his wedding someday.

"Adam. yaw my best fwend, but I shuuwa wished you wiked spowts."

"Adam, this is my fwend, Josh, Josh Weina, no seriously, it weally is weina."

Tommy was so pure that it wasn't offensive to his friend Josh that he found his last name unbelievable or funny. Tommy never meant anything in a mean spirit, it was never in him. He was always the nicest kid. He and Adam used to sit at the computer and make videos of themselves. This text he sent was to share one he rediscovered a few days earlier. It lifted me from the despondency as I laughed out loud.

It's a video of the two boys on a roller coaster. They had made it in Tommy's kitchen, on the Mac Photobooth app with a virtual background, interrupted by his dad, Rich, behind them doing dishes. This feature was one they had used a lot in 4th grade. They're in a roller coaster game show, taking turns playing host and contestant and asking silly questions. The contestant's right or wrong answers stop or start the roller coaster. This episode's content was typical immature boy humor, with toilet references and purposeful wrong answers. Now I was no longer sad.

Awake with my phone in my hands, I noticed other texts that had come through while I slept. All from Adam's friends - those I had assumed had forgotten him over the last year, and who, that very afternoon, I had also assumed I would not hear from again - individually reaching out.

Hi naomi! It's ella i'm not sure if you
remember me specifically but I was really close

friends with Adam. I just wanted to say how
thankful I am that you are so open to having us
over and talking about him in a positive sense
because that helps so much. I didn't want to
mention this today but there was one memory
of him that really really stuck with me. This
was two years ago and our entire friend group
was just hanging out one day in the woods (not
too sure why). I was really really stressed
because my mom was coming and everyone was
about to leave to go to mcdonalds but i had to
wait there for my mom. Anyways, I was telling
people to just wait 5 more minutes because I
didn't want to wait alone in the woods. Nobody
listened and just ran off. I was completely alone
and waiting on a rock by the road when Adam
walked back to me. Everyone else had already
left but Adam came back. he talked to me and
waited with me on that rock because he cared. I
have never in my life seen anyone with such a
big heart as that boy. After that night i made a
conscious effort to go out of my way and be
there for people who need it. Adam had so much
love in his heart and it is so so so so evident
that he made such a huge effect on every person
he met. That memory has stayed with me since
that day and I will never forget about that or
him. Thank you for being the mother of such an
amazing angel. Another thing I wanted to say
is that I am truly so sorry that my friends and I
haven't made more of an effort to stop in, I
really think the reason was that part of moving

on was kind of separating ourselves from his
death consuming our lives but i want you to
know that by NO MEANS he was forgotten or
will ever be. Speaking for myself I think about
him every day. Also, he is always remembered
when we have group hangouts and mentioned
because he still is such a significant part of all
of us. Thank you Naomi 🖤

Accompanying the text was a selfie of she and Adam and another face somewhat cut off. She explained further.

That's from the day he came back to the rock for
me. The girl next to him is Ava. She saw him
coming back to me and came back too.

> *Wow. What a gift this is. Thank you*
> *Ella. You were at my house on*
> *Halloween right?*

Yes

> *I remember you very clearly bc you*
> *were so expressive on Halloween.*
> *You looked in my eyes and it made an*
> *impression on me*
>
> *Thank you*

Thank you for saying that it means a lot 🖤 🖤

> *When the three of you left on*
> *Halloween i closed the door and broke*
> *down pretty bad. One of the worst*
> *fits of crying I've had. Mindy*

actually held and comforted me I was so broken down.

Over the past year I have been battling a loneliness bc I thought all of your lives had just moved on and he was slowly being forgotten. People kept saying it was not true but I could not get over the feeling. The way you three came to my door. And in particular the way your eyes looked so deeply at me on Halloween made that feeling go away. I hope forever. Because I hope all of you will stay close and keep reassuring me and sharing his beautiful memory.

Thank you so much for realizing that he could never ever be forgotten! Trust me, he is present in all of our lives. 🖤🖤🖤

Love it. Thank you. And remember to see the lives around you. Love you

I will 🖤🖤🖤

And more…

Hi Mrs. Brickel, It's Jamie. I was at your house today and last night. I thought you might want the video I showed you today

She shared a link to a video of a reluctant Adam in a dress being encouraged by his friends to twirl around in order for it to flow gracefully. He had arrived late at a gathering and been tricked into believing that all of the boys in the group had agreed to the same.

At this point I restoked the fire, poured a glass of wine and turned on the lights. The darkness was certainly lifting, and I was laughing out loud again.

*and this is the paragraph I wrote for him the
day after he died, which was when I found out*

She sent a screenshot of her Instagram post from that day:

*Its insane how quickly someone can be stripped
of their life, especially the people who deserve it
the least. Adam, you were such an amazing and
beautiful person and everyday seeing you and
just your smile and the way you say "hey"
would put a smile on my face. You make
everyone around you happy. Even when im
having a bad day, seeing you makes me happy.
you are such an angel and I know you are in
the best place right now, but i wish you could
still be here with everyone who loves you. I still
remember in sixth grade when I had a crush on
you and we became friends in Ms. Breslin's
and you sat in front of me because of our last
names and I would always think about how our
lives would be when we got married once we
were adults (because that's typically what sixth
grade girls think about when they have a crush)
and its crazy to think that you won't even be
here when we are older. but then again, you are
here, looking down on all of the people who love*

you, and you will always be here, right in our
hearts. rest well Adam, we'll meet again soon

♡

> *Thank you Jamie. You are such a beautiful*
> *girl. Adam was lucky to have you as a*
> *friend and I know he will help you find the*
> *perfect husband. He does things like that.*
> *Thank you so much for sharing this and for*
> *sharing this day with me. I'm so glad I*
> *have gotten the chance to know you. I will*
> *treasure your friendship and hope you will*
> *stay present in my life.*
>
> *And that video is priceless*

isnt it so funny?? also, that means so much to
me. im really sorry I havent stopped by this
past year (other than halloween) I was just
having a lot of trouble dealing with everything
and I didn't want to break down in front of you
or your family. I will be stopping by much more
often this year ♡

> *Listen. I may look strong but I cry every*
> *day. I fell asleep on my couch this*
> *afternoon and gotten woken up by this*
> *incredible sadness that life must go on.*
> *Then I saw your text and it made me feel*
> *good. Then I watched the video and*
> *laughed. All of these emotions are ok. I*
> *would rather have someone break down in*
> *front of me than think he was forgotten. So*
> *please feel ok to come and cry.*

Not to Spoil the Ending... but everything is going to be ok

And thank you for lifting me

The next day I got a text from Adam's friend Laura. She wanted to know if we could set up a time for all the friends to take me to dinner. Instead we arranged that they would all come to me on the 12th the following month, and they did. It blossomed into a monthly tradition where I have cooked dinner for however many of them could make it, each month. Sometimes it was 20, sometimes less, and it lasted until August, when, even in the middle of Covid the friends decided to organize an outdoor 'distanced' graduation for Adam before they headed off to college. Before they left that night we decided to make plans to continue the tradition over their school vacations. I know better now than to assume it won't happen.

I learned a valuable lesson from 16-year-olds in my darkest hour, and it has impacted me and changed my own behavior during Covid. I learned about stepping out to connect and comfort. When I contemplate how it would feel for me to reach out to a grieving mother I barely knew, offer comfort that might not be welcomed, I admit it's easier to only think about being kind, and let it end there rather than take a risk – it's easier to keep my kindness close and safe at home. But I now realize it's not better. I'm forever changed, and blessed that those kids had more courage in their kindness than I did. I've learned from a generation, often accused of being protected, enabled, and selfish, how to open my heart and step out courageously, loving generously.

The next morning I got more texts. Lots of pictures of feet with mismatched socks around the halls of NRHS, and even from a college campus halfway across the country. It was November 13, which I found out later that afternoon is actually

199

"International Kindness Day." Go Adam! And these kids, 16-year-olds, remembering, taking the time to connect. ...

They literally woke me from despair.

Minecraft

A few months ago, my mom started talking about what she considered exciting news in our Catholic faith, a millennial saint. New saints are a big deal. The process to sainthood means that the person has died, was noted in his life for being exceptional, and has since performed miracles that are "approved" according to complex administrative standards from Rome. It goes in stages, and this one had just cleared the first hurdle. Carlo Acutis died of leukemia in 2006. During his life he was drawn to sacred things and had a great love of Jesus and the Church. He was a computer genius who used his talents to do good religious things. Like Adam, he loved Minecraft. Interestingly, they shared similar features and good looks too, and they both died at 15.

Unlike Adam, Carlo went to church every single day and had great devotion to the sacraments, I heard in a homily at church one Sunday. As I sat listening, I remembered texts I had found on Adam's phone: texts where Adam asked Tommy which priest was saying the 5pm mass that Tommy was attending. Adam's question wasn't motivated by a desire to run over should it be someone inspiring, but by his need to have the right name when asked at Sunday dinner who'd said the mass that he told me he went to.

A few nights after hearing about this new young "almost saint," Fr. Frank, the priest who gave the homily was at my kitchen table having dinner.

"You seem excited about this Carlo Acutis guy." I pointed out, referring back to it.

"Oh yes. He's great. Isn't it amazing? I knew you'd like it. A young man, 15 years old. Like Adam!"

"Meh…"

To be perfectly honest, I was getting a bit sick of Carlo Acutis and his 15-year-old perfection. How much did I have to hear about a kid who was up in Heaven performing miracles and having a grand, old, loving time? Where did that leave Adam, the one who likely skipped church the night he died?

A few days later, exactly three years after Adam's death, I got a text:

Hi Naomi, this is Christophe, Adam's friend. I know you must get tons of messages about this, but I never reached out personally and I feel that I should have. I wanted to let you and the rest of Adam's family know I still think of Adam extremely often, and I miss him immensely. I'm so sorry he had to be taken so soon. Of course this is painful for me, but for you and your family, - even 3 years later, I cannot imagine how painful this time must be for you. Adam and I began slowly drifting apart the last 1-2 years of his life, not in a bad way, we just spoke less. Still, I always appreciated his friendship so much. I didn't have many friends growing up and Adam was one of the few people that at that age, I could

actually call a real friend. Like the card with his
picture, I try not to be sad that it ended, but
grateful that it happened. I will always be
grateful that I had the opportunity to have him
as a friend.

Christophe is the son of my friend Doug. He and Adam became close friends over a passion they shared for Minecraft. A few weeks after Adam died, I started to wonder about the Minecraft friends in cyberspace that I had heard Adam yelling at through his gaming headset for so many years. They would have no way of knowing why he just stopped coming on, no longer showed up, or "left the server."

It made me sick the more I considered it. I tried to go on his computer and see if I might somehow communicate with them, but the platform was beyond my tech savvy. I remembered that Christophe and Adam had enjoyed playing Minecraft together. Their sleepovers always entailed multiple trips back and forth to the car transporting monitors and gaming equipment. I decided to see if he could assist. Christophe came over, got on Adam's computer and was able to see the last person Adam played with. I asked him to leave a message for her with my phone number.

A few days later she called. Her name is Diane Flores. She was stunned when I told her the terrible news. She had wondered about him because he had said he would be back on later that night and never returned. There wasn't much else to say, but she promised to tell his friends in that world. He was really good at Minecraft she told me, and very loved.

I hung up feeling strange, and assumed she was as quickly gone as our call had lasted. This virtual friend, I knew nothing about her and would likely never hear from again. She had never even met him in person, and yet he had touched and connected with her. A few days later I got the following email:

From: Diane Flores
Subject: adam
Date: November 25, 2017 at 6:16:48 PM EST
To: Naomi Brickel

So I guess I should start out with the fact that Adam went by Brick online. Let me know if you have any questions about things that people said. I know there's some stuff about him involving minecraft. I should probably also mention that Solert is a multiplayer Minecraft vanilla server. Adam was probably one of the most active people on there. He was even elected Overlord of the server. Overlord is kind of like the president. We just named it overlord.

Here are some things that the people among our friend group said on our discord. You can probably scroll up the Solert discord in general chat and read other things on there.

Brick was such a great guy and I'm at a loss for words. I wanted to send a message tomorrow thanking everyone for everything because it would be Thanksgiving and all. But saying thank you is something I should've done a while ago. It's destroying me that I can't tell Brick what I'm saying now. There isn't a day that goes by that I'm not thankful for you guys. For your friendships. For playing together. Everything. I'm so proud to be a part of this community. You all are so special to me and I don't know how to express that other than by saying thank you. I'm going miss Brick so much. I already do. -Parker123101

Love your words Parker Hard to believe he's gone, but what we need to do now is to support each other and his family and loved ones, not question and hope that it's a joke. That only adds to the pain. Let's remember Brick and all the great times we had with him, and even though we wish he was still here I firmly believe he's happy, wherever he is, and he'd want us to be happy even though he's not here anymore. Love you Brick buddy, rest in peace. -Talon

Brick is the only reason im here and still have the joy of turning my computer and having some of the most fun of my life. He invited me to this community of you people who have changed the person who i am for the better. I was open to more experiences like trying other games or getting help for my own self. Brick had qualities i wish i had for myself. Brick was passionate about the server. His ideas and hardwork truly changed the server for the better. On the server he helped others do projects for more things to be completed. Brick worked and helped with the community projects as well. He wanted big changes on the server which is why he became overload and tried his best on more creations on the server. Brick also never let people walk over him and fought for what he believed in. He believed in himself in times when people could say he was acting foolish, and he stood his ground. In a way you were like a brickwall, you were standing your ground when people fought against you. Brick now resides in heaven where he plays now on his 1 million fps computer and lays in happiness, as he deserves for how well he has treated me, and probably many other people. Adam Brickel, I will NEVER forget you as every time I turn on my computer its due to you. Thank you for everything you provided me. Laughs inspiration, hardwork, confidence, and fun. - River

I didn't know Brick very well, but every time I joined the server, the teamspeak, the Discord, etc. he always was so friendly and even if I was being quiet (which is most of the time), he was always finding a way to keep the conversation going. He always knew how to brighten someone's day. I am very saddened by his passing. I'll miss him very much, and am very glad to have met him. The world was a much better place with him in it. -Jacey

Hey everyone, Happy Thanksgiving. This year's Thanksgiving was most definetly different than the rest as I not only spent it this year with different parts of my family, but I found out I lost a loved one the day before. As most of you know, most of my time is on the computer and such. The reason I spend so much of my time on the computer is because of the amazing friends I have all across the globe. Yesterday I found out one of my best friends Adam passed away due to heart failure. We met nearly 4 years ago on a server I helped out with and he was a member on there. After that server closed we became very close and even planned to meetup next year. Adam was only 15 years old and I treated him like a little brother. Adam was one of those people who was super motivated towards one thing and his passion towards that would rub off on me and get me super motivated towards something even if it was stupid. Events like this show me how much life throws you curveballs and you never know what will happen. Moral of the story is, even if someone is across the country, not family, etc, you should cherish the time you have with them because it might be the last.   *-TJ*

There were links to twitter feeds, and UHC reddit (whatever that is). There was art, a comic strip with Brick as the stunning brave hero. There were endless messages of how he had helped, inspired, motivated, cared. It went on and on. I tried to think of ways to pull it together so I'd always have access to it. I wept.

Adam was no Carlo Acutis. As my pastor, Fr. Thomas, put it in his homily at the funeral, "He was a normal teenager ..." but he was also "an extraordinary" teenager. I've come to realize through writing this, and through people like Christophe and Diane Flores, and everyone who's shared stories of his friendship, that Adam was an angel to many ... and maybe sainthood is simpler than the spiritual bureaucrats in Rome make it out to be. In fact, maybe Adam actually shared a devotion that was similar to Carlo. He was good to people, kind, passionate, encouraging, and loyal. What's more, he did his really good things in ordinary simple ways, without drawing attention. It's inspiring to think that it could be that easy, something we could all do without too much change or effort: small things, like noticing people, filling in the conversation to make them comfortable, standing by our friends and even helping them become their best selves. Where Carlo was drawn to the presence of God in the Eucharist, maybe Adam was drawn to the Holy Spirit of the Divine in all of the people he met. ...

Or maybe that's a mom talking ...

I hope Carlo actually made it, and is up there enjoying Minecraft with his new Overlord friend on a vanilla server on the 1 million FPS gaming computer. I'm sure he is. Lucky him, lucky Adam, lucky them, and lucky Heaven.

Oh, and Adam, PLEASE don't get Carlo in trouble! He's almost a saint!

An essay written by Adam's cousin, Claire, (10):

Who's Babysitting? *I've been begging my mom all day to tell me who is babysitting. She keeps saying that it is a surprise and if I keep guessing, she is just going to say maybe or no... Ding dong. "Adam." I say with the most excitement that I have had in my entire life. I keep asking him what we are going to do? My mom is just telling him what our bedtimes are. ... My parents finally left. ... Now the party really starts. We play games and it is perfect because most games can play only four people and there are four of us. Then his brother, Jude, his sister, Kit, and their dad, Doug, walked past with the dog named Kelly. We go outside and talk to them. Then we go to Adam's house and he makes vanilla milkshakes with almond extract. They were the best. He kept speaking Spanish to us. He was so funny. ... Family time is important. You should do something with your family and cherish it until the day life comes to an end.*

#IGotU

Adam. What a beautiful amazing human…. You once walked me all the way home when my mom was bugging me and nobody else would. We weren't even that close at the time, but that's just the kind of person you were. When I had nobody else to talk to, I would turn to you. You made a positive impact on so many people. Adam, I can promise you with everything in me that I will <u>NEVER</u> forget you. I love you so much. - ♥*Ella*

Adam was one of the sweetest boys we ever met, I remember this one time I was at the Lake Isle Fair all alone – and he took me over to the Barnes & Nobles and we spent like an hour going through all the joke books in the store. I will miss him dearly. ♥*Julia*

Adam had the kindest, most beautiful soul anyone could ever have. He was always there for you whether it was for an ear to listen or shoulder to cry on. Anytime I would pass by him in the hallway his huge smile would light up my face…. - Alissa C. ♥

Adam, thank you for being the sweetest, kindest and most thoughtful friend! I will never forget, one day I was absent from school and you came over to my lunch table and asked my friends where I was… You responded with "oh is she okay?" That is just the type of person you were…. Margaret DeR.

Adam, … I don't know how, but you always knew when there was something wrong with me, and we're able to comfort me and my times of need…. Thank you so much for being a ray of light in my life. I love you! ♥*Skyler*

211

I'm Happy and I'm Helping People

Text from Stacey Ramirez
11/24/17 12:48pm

*Ok-strange text! I've woken up the last few
days with a message from Adam. I've not
shared it because I didn't understand why he
would ask me, of all people, to give you a
message. But this morning his presence was
fading because I wasn't doing what he asked. I
promised I would text you today. Adam has
wanted me to tell you "I am happy and I'm
helping people." It was loud and clear the past
4 mornings. I'm sorry I didn't share it sooner. I
wasn't sure how you would take it and I
certainly don't want to cause you any more
hurt. I love you!*

> *Thank you very much. I truly believe that
> message is real bc he is helping people and
> I have felt his joy. Love u*

I'm so glad to hear you are feeling his joy.
That's exactly what I was hearing in his
message. Love!! 🦋

Thanks for sharing this. It was important

It was way out of my comfort zone. I'm old
enough to know that there are sometimes
unintentional consequences when my intent is
to help. I would never want to cause you more
pain.

It was important you shared and I am and
will be forever grateful for it

I love you

I was recently contacted by David, a colleague who I barely know. I've spoken to him once before over the phone. When he phoned initially, a year after Adam's death, it was to interview me as a potential candidate for a job. In our conversation, he asked about the greatest challenge I had faced in my work career, and though the job did not turn out to be a fit, the question inspired a deep and poignant conversation about the year following Adam's death, and my efforts to maintain my professional drive, purpose, and focus.

When he called this time, two years later, it was not about my career, but on behalf of another professional acquaintance who suddenly lost her child. He was uncertain and felt he might be breaking professional boundaries or that I might be upset or offended, but took the risk and called anyway. Moved by my resilience and outlook when we spoke the first time, he asked if I might be willing to speak with his friend. Of course I would, and I acknowledged his courage in reaching out. We ended up engaged in another conversation about friendship, being there for others, kindness, and the mysteries of life. It would be nice to meet him in person someday, we've clearly impacted one another in our limited phone interactions.

The call gave me so much to think about after. I'm writing during Covid, and death and mourning are strange "never before" experiences now. A friend's dad died recently and there was no wake, no funeral, no big Irish celebration of life with tears and singing. My friend was not even able to gather with family. Human history evidences that we are not intended to fly solo in those first days, weeks, and even months after the death of a loved one. Cultures have developed detailed communal ceremonies and traditions around death. As David and I spoke on the phone about his friend, I was pained at the thought of her by herself, and the idea of experiencing Adam's death under such circumstances. The pandemic has separated us from one another in ways we could never have conceived, and I could not imagine going through such a tragedy alone. In light of this, I was inspired by David's courage, and his actions to stay connected with her and provide comfort. I was moved and uplifted by such conscious, compassionate behavior.

A few months before Adam died, I bumped into Kirsty in the grocery store parking lot (the same Kirsty who would be there in the street that night we found him). We hadn't seen each other and caught up. She mentioned how handsome Adam had gotten, and, more importantly, that he was such a good kid. She shared a story about a night that summer. The kids had been hanging out, were drinking, and a girl decided to walk home. When Adam realized she was leaving alone he accompanied her the whole walk to her house. When he returned later, he unassumingly said it was nothing, it just wouldn't have been good for her to be by herself.

"You have a good boy. Who knows what might have happened to that girl all alone so late after drinking." Kirsty noted.

I agreed. I drove home feeling good about the young man he was turning into, even as our relationship changed. There was something that took some thought, effort and time away from the fun; Adam's own, deliberate charity.

The kindness, empathy, generosity and thoughtfulness of people were bright lights in the darkness of Adam's death. As I look back and reflect on the people in my kitchen those first few days and for months after, many of them had very little in common. They were men and women (the Sunset Crew was all female, I think), black, brown, and white, gay and straight, Catholic, Muslim and Jewish, Republicans and Democrats, but all were united in the love and desire to care for and comfort my family, my kids, my husband, and me, and in the purposeful way they acted with kindness. I bet most those "do gooders" barely recall their efforts. My everyday responsibilities got done, and our trauma was softened by their presence and small favors. There were rarely evenings I was alone. When people were around I could laugh, get out of my head, and, if only temporarily, enjoy respite from the darkness. Each of those kind deeds, big or small - from a birthday weekend with friends organized by my sister, to frequent texts from my sister-in-law, Hope, "On my way to the store, need anything?" shared a common, deliberate action, a choice, an acted upon compassion. And it made it all a little bit lighter.

We are living in dark times. The country is in a state of angst and toxicity. The tension and angry energy that surrounds politics is unlike any ever experienced in our country, at least in my memory. People are unraveling in the isolation of the pandemic. I am amazed at the agitation and anger in people I come across in my work, in the car, and even the grocery store. We live in a time where ugly behavior is highlighted in the media, and easily instigated in otherwise nice people. We are able to be connected and stay in touch with one another through iPhones, Facebook and ways that didn't exist ten years ago, and yet "social media" is an oxymoron. Dialogues in these platforms provide the worst examples of adult bullying. People are anxious, isolated, angry, aggressive, and so lonely.

And yet, I learned from the kindness bestowed on us following Adam's death, that each one of us is on the cusp of a heavenly world, one deliberate action, one choice away from making it all better, connecting with another, comforting someone lonely, or making a person who's depressed laugh. It's as simple as an invitation for dinner or a walk, or a Facetime to a friend "in quarantine." Maybe it's bigger - a courageous phone call like David's, or going to a friend's house in the middle of the night so he isn't alone after the trauma of his brother's shocking death; or seemingly nothing, like showing up the next morning with the Dunkin Donuts, so a grieving mom doesn't have to worry about breakfast. Perhaps it is unassumingly noticing and being there like Beth, or sending a thoughtful note to someone you barely know telling them you are pained for their loss, and that you keep their child's memory alive in the prayers with your young children, or sending a text saying, "Yo, where are we drinking" to your grieving friend … .

… Or a selfless quick decision to walk a drunk girl home.

I worry how anyone gets through their own shocking crises without being supported by the charity we were soaked in. I know that most people are not blessed with networks as large as mine. Those ideas and details have inspired me to be more courageous in my outreach to others who are suffering. The seemingly disconnected actions articulated above share a common and powerful antidote, even for the current pain that engulfs our world.

Adam would sometimes interrupt moments of mean-spiritedness around him. I can picture sitting at our dinner table, Jude teasing Mindy, Mindy opening her mouth to say something angry and mean in response, and Adam interjecting, "Minnndy? Niiiiice?" A simple (albeit playful, teasing, and of course annoying to Mindy) reminder to let go of anger for kindness from the kid who took all the blankets to create a soft bed on the hard floor for his dog, walked a drunk girl home, and touched a sad kid in Chemistry class. Adam was onto something, like David, and all those who lightened our burden in those bleak days, like Beth, and like Nancy, Tina, Lloyd, Yvette and Mark, Arianne, Kath, and countless others. Their examples impacted me, and now I am more likely to act, rather than just feel. Such simple things have incredible power to change everything - a conscious, deliberate, and compassionate code of conduct.

I only met Adam this year in Spanish. I'm a freshman and I felt very uncomfortable in every one of my classes but Spanish, all because of Adam ... he would walk in with a giant smile on his face and it made me feel welcome when I didn't know anyone. ... Another thing Adam would do is write on the chalk or smartboard very large and would add things such a smiles in his O's and hearts in his I's. I didn't know Adam as well as others but I wish I did, he was a giant help for me to adjust to the high school.... from Joseph DeL. (9th grade)

Wow. Really. Could it be that simple? ... What's one thing I can do today?

Trampoline Thank You

Dear Dunn, Kirk, McCreery, Hickey, Anselmo, Baker, Best, Blair, Briscoe, Brown, Burrell, Carlin, Chandra, Ciscone, Collins, Connolly, Cremins, Croker, Cunningham, D'Ablemont-Smith, Deutsch, Eaton, Fama, Fanning, Feeley, Fleming, Flood, Fullerton, Gallagher, Glennon, Castelitto-Gil, Annie Glennon, Chad Glennon, Grimes, Haley-Silvers, Handler, Harris, Harshman, Hartley, Jennings, Keefer, Lloyd, LoConte, Lynch, Magarelli, Manley, Mannix, McMillan, Millette, Morris, Nascimento, Nason, Nordquist, O'Connell, O'Shea, Chris Pace, Rich Pace, Patricot, Payne, Kirk Palmer, Phil Palmer, Ranje, Rice, Ridder, Rizzo, Robinson, Ruggiero, Smith, Sullivan, Sweeney, Tomei, and Vasandani families... phew

I have sat to write this so often, but each time gotten too overcome with every possible emotion to follow through. Wow! Thank you! I don't even know how to express the gratitude we feel over this huge kindness in our precious Adam's memory! How fitting a tribute a new, working trampoline is to the memory of a boy who was so filled with fun, joy, and kindness - especially to younger children on his old broken-down trampoline. (I have so many memories looking out at him bouncing while enjoying friends and cousins.) And that amazing gift would have been beyond generous, but in addition, such a donation with it! I have not decided what to do with the monetary proceeds of all of your

219

goodness, but I am waiting for Adam to direct me how best to use it to most appropriately cherish his memory. Thank you!

During this time, I have learned that blessings actually shine brighter during the darkest hours; and amidst this sadness, I still can feel joyful contemplating them - lessons, signs and messages from Adam, deep experiences of love and support from friends (and even people we did not know), new but already cherished friendships developed directly out of this experience, and on and on ... I have learned a lot about being there for others in their suffering, even stepping out of my comfort zone to do so, from the comfort we received from all of you and so many! This may seem exaggerated, but from where I'm experiencing things, the world actually seems to be a nicer place today than a month ago. I guess that is just one more blessing.

Please send your kids to our new trampoline! Let us see them jumping and screaming and laughing. Help us as we create new memories watching Jude enjoy his friends and younger (and older) neighborhood kids and cousins. If you really know me you know I'm not much of an enforcer, however, in Adam's memory I do ask only for the acknowledgment of a few simple rules listed on the next page.

We are so grateful for the love and kindness you all have shown our family. We ask that you continue to pray for us, and not to be shy about reaching out to check in. I cannot express sufficiently how much it means, and how deeply comforting it has been to feel the love and support that has been offered.

With most sincere love and thanks,

Naomi - and the entire Brickel family

Adams Trampoline Rules

Love

Joy

Peace

Patience

Kindness

Goodness

Faithfulness

Gentleness

Self-control

*Compliance encouraged but not required – All Welcome

~

The new trampoline did not just show up randomly in a box. It arrived on the 12th of December, the one-month anniversary of his death. While I was distracted upstairs by friends, it was fully assembled by two men from the store where it had been purchased. I wonder if they knew the poignant memorial significance of this assembly? I wonder if they realized, as they lugged away the old one, that they were disposing of what, in the schemes and mechanisms of my religion, one might consider "a relic?"

In Catholicism, as I mentioned previously, saints are canonized after a lengthy man-made and institutionally prescribed process, and then their "stuff" becomes important. To be declared, that is canonized, "saint" means that the Church has deemed you made it. No more waiting and suffering, no further restitution for sins committed. You're in. You've crossed the Pearly Gate finish line, and can enjoy your castle in the clouds (and in Adam's case unlimited candy and all-you-can-eat bakery). Things that the saints used a lot, especially in the actions of their faith, like their bibles, rosaries, maybe a chalice for a priest, even a cane, are considered "second class relics," and are cherished for their own, I guess, aura.

Adam lived a Spirit-inspired existence. Evidence suggests he's floating around the heavens continuing his earthly good works from the next dimension. As his mom, chief advocate for the cause, and official collector of the stories of his life and "ministry," including joy-filled visitations, signs, and the "don't worry, it's gonna be ok" messages similar to Jesus' own frequent directives, "Do not be afraid," etc., I'm confident: "Saint Adam," or more precisely, "St. Adam Martin Pope John Paul II Brickel." He performed acts of kindness and his best thinking on the trampoline. According to my religious faith knowledge, some inferences, and a bit of a stretch, that old broken-down trampoline might just classify as a second-class relic, and is perhaps lying in a landfill somewhere trying to be miraculous.

During Adam's life, the dangerous broken trampoline was a regular part of his routine. When he wasn't at school, baking, sleeping, or in the shower, Adam spent a lot of time at my desk in the living room (most still refer to it as Adam's desk) playing Minecraft. Minecraft is not just another video game measuring reflexes and hand-eye dexterity. For Adam at least, it was also an intense mental exercise. As he played he would develop and stick post-it notes with codes and IP addresses around the computer screen. I could never decipher it, but know it wasn't simple. He would simultaneously coordinate people over his headset the whole time, "River, River, River, spot me!"

or "I got you, Parker", etc. There were certain names I became familiar with.

After more extreme strenuous games, he would often pop up from his seat at the desk and walk purposefully to the door, run out to our deck, up onto the picnic table, across to the railing, and launch, up, across, and over the protective netting onto the trampoline, in literally five steps. He would land and continue to bounce high and with vigor in order to let off steam. He also spent a lot of time there wrestling fiercely and playing an aggressive ball pegging type game with his brothers and friends; and bouncing gently and kindly with his younger cousins and neighbors. The trampoline was a big part of all of our lives.

When Adam died, the trampoline was ten years old. Some moms had prohibited their children from bouncing on it. I should have. I purchased it with my first paycheck when I went back to work after being home for several years as I raised the kids. I returned when the youngest, Jude, was three. It was not an easy transition for any of us, though I came to appreciate quickly the affirmation that comes in the workplace, which moms at home are far less likely to experience. It was a welcome change to have my work recognized and valued, and to see the fruits of my efforts celebrated, as responsibilities and salary simultaneously increased. This was a first for me. Moms are not generally acknowledged in this way. More often than not, they are questioned about how they are doing things, or what they did all day, and dump even more on themselves about their overall value to the home "organization." There is no stay-at-home-mom ladder, or opportunities to feel like you've made it. You start at the beginning, that first day you bring your new baby home, brand new parent, frightened and clueless. Each day poses new dilemmas, new insecurities about your proficiency, no opportunity to become cocky in your expertise as the issues they impose increase in complexity with their age. Then they are teenagers, making you quite sure, with their intense reinforcement, that you chose the wrong career, because, as a mom, you suck.

The decision to go back to work, while providing a break from the self-doubt at home, added new self-questioning. While a day at the office was less work than a day at home, the respite came with a hovering awareness of all that was waiting when I walked in that evening, a tugging at the heart for the things I could be doing at home, and the reckoning from the kids themselves. My children were not happy with the new job for mom, so I decided to reinforce the benefits of mom working, surprising them with this wonderful new yard toy. They arrived home one day to an assembled trampoline in the yard. All were elated. We got our money's worth, and so did the neighbors and all my kids' friends. It was fun. It was one of the best investments we ever made.

So, to honor Adams' memory, a new working trampoline for the Brickels was a glorious and much appreciated way to send love and express condolences. I'm ever grateful to all of the families that participated. I sometimes go out there myself to let off steam. It's great exercise and a wonderful release. And, as my thank you letter requested, the kids did come. Almost every day I would look out through the windows and see kids bouncing. It lifted my otherwise heavy heart and made me smile. Certainly, the intentions of those who had been so generous were fulfilled.

~

There was a small group of girls who became trampoline regulars. One was Adam's cousin Claire; the others, Ellie, Chloe,

Sophia and Ella all lived in the neighborhood. Ella is the younger sister of Lili Mae, who had been first on the scene that terrible night. The girls were all in 5th grade like Jude. For them, Adam, a sophomore in high school, had been older, cool, kind and someone they had looked up to. As much as they loved to jump on the trampoline, there was something else that drew them to our yard. Someday Jude may revel in the idea that it was him. As the youngest in a big family in a neighborhood with more and more younger families with kids moving in, Jude was fortunate to have many friends nearby. When he went to kindergarten there were so many others his age that they added a new bus route for the neighborhood. Most were girls (this will likely plague me soon, more than it did in his years of prepubescent annoyingness).

Jude gained an aura as the sibling of their babysitter and a big kid they looked up to. He naturally fit in and enjoyed being social. As the youngest of six, he's an old soul, "a 16-year-old at birth," both in his maturity and lack of it.

Jude was also a wanderer. The Brickel "leash" had worn out before he was born. We live on a formulation of three intersecting streets, encompassing 15-20 houses that are accessible through backyards without crossing a street (important for an explorer under five). From the time he could walk, he always loved roaming the "island," as we called our block. He visited all of the inhabitants, whether I'd met them or not, and got to know and share all of our mutual (or not) business.

One day stands out when he was three or four, in springtime. Jude went out, and I didn't think much about it. After a while I realized I hadn't seen him. I called the Sullies and Pace's, his usual stops, but there were no recent sightings. My fears arose and I went out anxiously to find him, "Jude!

Juuude!!" Nervously, I ran out to the street side of a neighbor's house, the same front yard where years later I would experience the real tragedy. Several neighbors had nannies who'd taken advantage of the beautiful day to congregate with the kids entrusted to them. Jude was among them, entertaining the babysitters more than playing with the kids.

"Jude! My gosh, I've been looking for you!" I said sternly.

"Are you Jude's mom?" One of the nannies asked. Many of the nannies in our neighborhood were from abroad, here to experience the states and learn English.

"Hi. Yes. Jude! You can't just go in front yards without telling me!"

"Oh. He is so cute! We love Jude! So friendly. We call him, how do you call it, Tom Sawyer? Haha, because he is always alone, and never shoes! He has beautiful hair!"

… Jude was friendly and popular with hair out of classic literature, and I was mom of the year.

~

I do think the girls showing up in our yard on the new trampoline held something more nuanced than Jude's popularity and friendliness. They seemed drawn to our home, our family, to Jude (but for different reasons), and to me, Adam's mom. They would come to the door with something to tell me, frequently they came in for drinks or snacks. They got comfortable sitting at my table talking about school, telling me Jude stories, laughing and being silly, and sharing and hearing Adam memories, including our prank phone calls.

I used to wonder what attracted them. Perhaps a need to nurture. Jude definitely had friends surround him more closely in the aftermath. There were stories of really nice, straight-laced kids actually getting into trouble, sometimes even fights, in their efforts to protect him from kids who talked about Adam on the playground (Jude hated when anyone talked about it), or even teased him about his dad or dead brother.

People, these kids included, had a need to comfort us. Perhaps too, it provided reassurance to experience what it was like in our house, to see that we were not outwardly anguished and traumatized (even if we were privately) and we would make it, despite the horrible tragedy that had befallen us. Adam's death, someone they knew and saw every day, would have been unsettling and scary, especially for young kids trying to figure life out. I think they liked being comfortable in our home, seeing we were ok, and even helping to ensure that we were. I loved that they wanted to be here, and as I drove home from work, I looked forward to walking in the door and seeing them around our table with Jude. I started to order more snacks and juice.

These kids will all be nothing but trouble one day, and I've loved watching it all develop. I feel privileged having some inside scoop.

Adam@havefundogood.co

Just a few days before my "Soulshine" experience in Westhampton, I got a call from my pastor, Fr. Thomas. Adam was clearly around that week.

"Hi! I was thinking about you! How's it going?" I asked as I answered his call.

"Hello my friend. I'm well. I'm well. But, how are you?" He asked.

"I'm hanging in, not bad. Things are busy here." There's no point in laying on the reality after a while. "Busy" became my auto-response.

"I just have to tell you about this weird thing that happened to me this morning. I got the strangest email. I have no idea what it is, I looked it up afterwards and can't imagine how I got on the distribution list, but it was an email from, get this, "adam@havefundogood.com." So weird, after the conversations this weekend about him. It is some sort of a group for young people who get together socially, they even drink beer, and do volunteer projects. I really have no idea how it could have gotten to me, well, except from him!"

He forwarded the email. I saved it. How does that happen? I still chuckle thinking about it.

Six months later, early on Adam's 16th birthday I got another email from Fr. Thomas. I was anxious at first. He was planning to say a mass to commemorate the day. It was Adam's first birthday after his death, and needless to say, a tough milestone. I worried he was backing out.

After a long hiatus, the Adam email is
back... And of all days —-today

Sent from my iPhone

He again forwarded an email he had gotten from Adam@havefundogood.com, on Adam's birthday. What a strange wonderful sign, and what a cool way for Adam to emphasize the messages of his life for all of us, and his presence on his 16th birthday.

At some point I became tempted to email whoever this Adam was and went to open the email and look at the address again. As I looked this time, I noticed that the return email was actually not complete. It ended with a ".co" rather than the typical ".com." Something about that made me not attempt to add the "m" myself, and instead leave it, accepting it simply for what it had been for Father, for me, and for Adam, a perhaps over-obvious reminder to have fun and do good.

I try to smile more now, especially at work. If someone asks me a favor, and I agree, I try to appreciate and even be grateful for the opportunity, smile through it, enjoy the connection with this person, rather than let myself become aware of a burden in the request. Have you ever stopped to notice how you feel when you are doing something nice for someone? I've become more mindful of it; I actually feel happy, fulfilled. If we don't enjoy our opportunities for generosity, it might just be better to avoid them, take care of oneself, forget others. If we're not happy in our assistance, if we feel burdened, put out, overextended, then let's face it, they know; and we are probably doing more harm than good. Why add more to a person's load who needed it lightened in the first place when they asked?

This morning, I got a text from my 16-year-old niece, Brennan. Brennan is the cousin next in age after Adam, three years younger. She's now older than Adam was when he died. Her 16th birthday was as poignant for me as Adam's own, the first one he was not here for. Here is the text she sent at 7:35am on her way to school.

I saw someone this morning whose
name was Adam and his shirt said do
good - I totally thought of you and
Adam 💚

Have fun and do good. Thanks for the reminder, Brennan. I will definitely remember that today.

That Black Life Matters

When I take my walks around town I see a lot of plastic signs. I suspect one of the unintended and unforeseen consequences of the Covid pandemic will be a glut of plastic and the issue of how to dispose of it. Prior to Covid, we had gained momentum in environmental consciousness. Plastic bags were practically outlawed, even paper was an extra charge. People were tuned in and deliberate about cleaning up our oceans, being "green" and the reduction of plastic waste.

It all seems to have become a secondary casualty of the pandemic. During those first few months of "stay at home," I took long walks every day. A suburban phenomenon I witnessed was that, perhaps in people's lack of ability to see and speak to one another, and still having a need to be heard, they used lawn signs. These small but substantial placards on metal spikes are still stuck into some front lawns and curbsides. Previously used primarily to indicate political support in elections, they became prolific, utilized to communicate the one thing each home was burning to share. They popped up showing pride for a graduate, thanks to the sanitation collectors, a shout out of support and encouragement for "essential workers," reminders to "wear your mask" or "social distance," and the assertion that "Black Lives Matter."

I am writing this in unsettling times. The world is still on pause due to the pandemic. My youngest, Jude, has not gone back to school except for a few random days where he sits in empty classrooms while his teachers teach to the kids at home on zoom. The presidential elections and transition passed, marking the most divisive race ever. The capital was stormed in the changeover because the loser couldn't leave gracefully. Covid infection rates climbed all winter. Cities across the country were burned and looted last summer during riots associated with police shootings of black men. It's scary.

I am not a political person, at all. I know, that's easy to say. Everyone is political, right? Every person has a view, lately polar, on one side or another. But I'm really not. I'm not going to go into it, because if I did I would actually be sharing my individual politics, and I'm really, seriously, not into it. I'm probably one of the few people, at least around me, who had to actually thoughtfully consider: Trump or Biden. Uh Oh. You've Googled me. "Not a political person? You're full of it. Look at your job." How is someone who coordinates organizational public policy initiatives not political? It's true that I'm very involved in policy issues, and I have been very involved in education and disability policy, especially in New York State. On a day-to-day basis, I interact with legislators and policymakers for my work. This brings me in touch with Republicans and Democratic legislators and those who make the laws in the state departments.

To be perfectly candid, I'm a registered Democrat. My line of work, and my passion in that work, steer me left. The simple reality is that Democrats tend to be more focused on those issues than Republicans. But when I say I'm not political what I mean is I'm not really heavily directed either way, and I'm not "on a side." CNN or Fox? Neither, too biased, "fake news."

While I read presidential candidates' political platforms on disability policy because of my work, I couldn't stomach the conventions or debates. I avoid strong judgements, because I don't spend enough attention to form an opinion. I walk away from conversations at the dinner table. So, to touch this is probably thorny...

The "Black Lives Matter" movement gained great momentum over the last year. It's a topic that gets attention in my work, at dinner, and on the lawn signs I walk by. The issues are real, but I bemoan the obvious question: Why, after all of this time, do we need this movement? How are we here in the 21st century United States of America, almost over 150 years after slavery, 70 years after the Supreme Court declared segregated schools unconstitutional, with things still so racially unbalanced? I'm not disputing that the systems are lopsided and disadvantage people of color, but it can't be that white people don't care. I see the signs. I witnessed protests in my homogeneous beach town. People didn't have to, but they made the effort. Last summer after the George Floyd riots, I received more emails than I could count from companies whose contact lists I'm on, insisting, "We do not tolerate ..."

Don't misinterpret my questions for any lack of support of the issues or movement. My work priorities in education involve real issues of disproportionate representation of minorities in disciplinary proceedings, suspension, disability labels, etc. I know that the majority of black children in our country go to schools made up only of other minorities. While I'm white, I have people I am very close to who have lived the reality first hand. Adam had black cousins (my own cousins' kids). I see the issues daily; they're real and I am fully behind much needed change. But there's something missing. And to be perfectly frank, there are aspects that feel more superficial than meaningful, like emails from corporations with little or no diversity and executive suites that could be mistaken for a cocktail lounge in an exclusive country club. Some of it strikes me somewhat "fake," as Adam would've put it. Perhaps I'm overly focused on the outward, staged actions around the collective issue, but it all seems to lack a real or individual relevance, recognition and tangible relationship to actual black people and personal lives. As good, important and welcomed as our collective advocacy is, I don't see the human connection, which I think is critical for meaningful change. So why do I bring this up? Of all the issues to "not be political" about?

Adam, and Corey.

Corey is a large, strong, gentle, young black man with a big inviting smile. He went to school with Adam starting in middle school and told me that Adam was his close friend. When I first met Corey his black hair was in long braids. I saw him after the state championship game without them, sporting a magnificent out of control 'fro. This year, as a senior, Corey was the captain of the New Rochelle High School NYS Championship football team. He went off to study at the prestigious NYU this fall. He is most of all humble, but also smart, kind, well-loved, and a leader. He is not the only black kid that claimed Adam as a close friend. There were many, but in addition to Corey I have also become close to two others - Jaiden and Derek. Jaiden was a year older than Adam. His last name is the same as ours, except for a minor difference in spelling. He became close to Jude and texts him often. He also texts me sweet messages and emoji hearts on important days, like Christmas, Adam's birthday, Mother's Day, etc., and Adam was his "great friend." I have more recently gotten to know Derek, even though he was always present at the house on the anniversaries and important days. He's quieter, and we never spoke until this summer, but he is now a son to me. After revealing that he lost his mom when he was very young, we decided together we could both fill a role (and a hole) for the other. He's a tall handsome guy. What he has repeated to me about Adam was that he was so kind. He sat behind Adam in math, and once told me that weeks after he died a new student came into the class and sat unaware in Adam's empty seat. "I just couldn't let him be in Adam's place. I had to tell him to move." Derek is well over 6 feet and 240 lbs., and I can only imagine the anxiety that poor kid felt being redirected in his mistake. But it truly amazes me how all of these big strong "heroes" were so moved by Adam's friendship.

They are all very dear to me, but there was something special about how my relationship with Corey developed. He's been generous in showing care and concern for me, and has a wonderful family. His mom and grandmother accompanied him to the visitation when Adam died. His grandmother, who also lost a child, wrote me a beautiful note that I still have. It felt so generous at the time for her to come to the house of someone she didn't even know, a friend of her grandson's. She certainly could have just as easily not.

But it isn't his good upbringing or even his wonderful qualities that made Corey so dear; it's the way that Adam has managed to find his way to me through him. He often connects, out of the blue, when I am struggling or feel sad. A lift at the right time, as if a little wave from Adam. He reached out to me last January right before Covid, and right before my birthday:

Hi Mrs. Brickel, I hope all is well. I was
thinking about you and just wanted to let you
know how much you mean to me. I am truly
blessed and thankful to have you in my life.

Hi Corey. I'm feeling very blessed by your outreach. What made you do it tonight? I've been having a tougher time lately. And feeling Adam poke in sometimes. Just wondering if this is connected.

You are an impressive man. I'm proud Adam knew you and relished your friendship. I got to watch (your team captain leadership) lately and was impressed by how you rose above all the bad adult behavior. I hope you will stay close to me. Please know this outreach is a gift in a hard time. And so I know Adam sent you.

I've been a little bit stressed out lately about the future and then today I heard the news of Kobe Bryant passing and it kind of put things in perspective.

Kobe hit me hard too

I realized how fortunate I am for the people that I have in my life so I wanted to reach out and let people know that I am thankful for them

And you are definitely one of those people

So this week is my birthday. And Adam always sends a person for special days. Something tells me it's you for this birthday. So can we plan a time to meet for coffee, or you come to dinner on Thursday, or something??

238

I feel like you could be a good fit for Jude
now too ... And he could always use
another big brother

I would love to come! I really appreciate your
kind words and of course I will look out for
Jude, he is family now.

It wasn't a big party. My mom cooked dinner, I got home from work late. So, it was just my mom, Mindy, Jude, Johnny, his friend Ish, Corey, and me. It was a nice night with the boys. We sat around my mom's family room and the kids got talking about their siblings, friends, and teachers in common. One of the teacher conversations prompted me to ask Corey,

"Didn't you have Mr. S. too? You were in the same classes with Adam in middle school, right?"

"No. We didn't have any classes together in middle school," he responded.

"Oh, I didn't realize it was high school. I thought for some reason you guys went back to middle school."

"Adam and I never had any classes together, but, yes, Adam was my close friend in middle school. He was actually my first friend."

"Oh?"

"Yes. I should have gone to Isaac (the other middle school in New Rochelle), but I went to Albert, and I didn't know anyone there. I sat alone at my own table in the lunchroom and Adam came and sat with me every day. It was just the two of us. That's how we became friends."

"Oh, wow. I don't think I knew that story, Corey. Wow. That's nice."

I excused myself lest my tears make the boys feel awkward.

It seems that Adam had a way of noticing, and was onto something critically important in how he maintained an awareness of individual persons, those that others missed. It would be furthest from the truth to suggest he didn't see color. One thing all of my kids agree to is that attending a diverse high school like New Rochelle's does not make you "not see color." On the contrary, the kids all see color; they notice and appreciate it. It's one of the things they value most even after they graduate. Beyond all of the academic, athletic, and extracurricular opportunities that were offered because of its sheer size, my kids would all point to the rich cultural and racial diversity as the part of New Rochelle High School they appreciate most.

Adam was known for speaking to people in their own "dialect." If you were Black, he talked AAVE (African American Vernacular English); Brown, "Spanglish," telemarketers from India were mimicked back. It might sound insensitive, even politically incorrect, but those who knew him, or were the target of this kind of attention were not offended. Adam was too authentic, inclusive, genuine, and kind to ever judge a person by their skin, faith, or culture. He loved to prank, loved to entertain and make people laugh, and it didn't rub people the wrong way because it was offered within the space of a real connection - and laughter.

In Kit's eulogy, she referred to a story from Adam's Spanish teacher. The story reflects this attribute perfectly. It was December, almost a full year before Adam died and we were all sitting around our kitchen table eating dinner. The phone rang, and I picked it up.

"Hi, Mrs. Brickel, this is Dr. Rodriguez. Adam's Spanish teacher. Is this Mrs. Brickel?"

"It might be." (No. I really didn't say that, but it was definitely the tone I used when I responded, "Yes." Calls from teachers did not generally mean good news in either the house I grew up in, or the one within which I was raising my kids.) I walked outside, so that the whole family would not hear me listening to whatever Adam was in trouble for.

"Mrs. Brickel. Nothing is wrong. I am happy to be making this call. I am really just calling to tell you what a wonderful boy Adam is, and how much I enjoy having him in my class. Your son Adam has given me hope in the future and in young people. In these past years I've become worried about the kids. I have seen so many changes. But having Adam in my class this year has given me back my hope. He makes us all laugh. He is so kind to everyone. Every kid loves him no matter what the race or background, and whether they are friends or not, he is everyone's friend."

Wow this was unusual. I was a bit stunned. I had never gotten a call like this ...

"I'd like to tell you a story. It's a little bit different, but shows the type of impact Adam has. I have another student in the class, a young woman. She is strong, almost tough sometimes. The other day, she came into class late and Adam was sitting in her seat. She was not in a good mood, and she went over and stood over him. She told him to move. Class had already started, so the attention of everyone was on this situation. It felt a little tense.

"He looked up at her, and using this slang affect that he uses, he said, 'Yo (name of girl,) you gotta lighten up, man, you gotta stop ackin so grumpy.' I stopped teaching. I couldn't believe it. All the kids in the class were watching. I felt nervous about how she might respond. But you know what she did? She just looked down at him and laughed, and she grabbed him, hugged him, and said, 'You're crazy Adam! I love you!!' And the whole class laughed.

"It was amazing, Mrs. Brickel, I didn't teach class. I needed to let the kids revel in and appreciate the moment. You have a very special boy. A very special kid. And he's so funny!"

So, without being political ... I think Adam was onto something important, perhaps the needed game-changer in this too slow-moving equity movement. It is one thing to be supportive of the collective, both important and necessary. But, we need to also remember that "Black Lives Matter," is about actual individual real black people, and the personal connection is equally, if not more, important and powerful as we strive towards meaningful change.

Adam had a way of seeing the person - black, brown, white or whatever - and being aware of their situation. He might notice and even bring playful attention to the details that differentiated them, but all within a relationship that was authentic and real; and that made it ok, and genuine. He wasn't a prophet or community activist, but he was "real." Those with whom he came in contact knew their individual lives actually mattered to Adam.

Maybe that is something that youth see better, or the adults have lost in our zeal. Perhaps it's as simple as noticing that black life alone at the lunch table, or the brown life looking sad at his desk in Chemistry class, and going over and connecting with the person, that individual life that matters.

#FAKE

Adam was always the one person I could talk to about anything.
Whether it was about shoes, girls, or just messing around, we always
seemed to connect. Although, one thing that Adam was always great
at was showing and telling me how to be a better person. If he ever
saw that someone was being a "fake" friend, he would call them out
and tell him to stop. He would also call someone out for just being a
mean person in general. He showed me that you should always put
yourself in someone else's shoes and look at things from a different
perspective, which is something I think will always stick with me.
Adam really means the world to me and I am so glad that I was able
to have such a strong relationship with him and be a part of the group
of people that he loved and has now inspired. I know for a fact that he
has made me, everyone in CWG, and all the other friends and family
better people. If it wasn't for Adam and all of the awesome times I've
had with him, I would 100% have a completely different view on the
people and world surrounding me. ... Love, Tommy F.

One theme I heard repeatedly came from Adam's close "CWG"
friends. They noted his authenticity, and how he valued that
quality in his friends and within relationships. Adam seemed to
see people in their fully developed humanity, rather than as a
limited means to an end or useful pawn in the game of life and
relationships; and that quality seemed to resonate the most
among the boys he was closest too.

Tristan

Tristan was one of Adam's very close friends who I never knew when Adam was alive. He was part of Adam's "inner circle." Adam had so many friends across so many groups that I hate to even use the phrase; it sounds too exclusionary, and so not Adam. So many have told me he was their "best friend" and they don't all necessarily know one another. There was a particular group of guys, though, that Adam spent a lot of his time with, "CWG." Tristan was one of them.

I got to know Tristan around the anniversary when the kids began to become a part of my life. Tristan had things he wanted to share with me that day, important ways Adam had impacted him while he was alive, and since. As people were leaving the anniversary gathering at my house, he asked if he could speak to me alone. I was a little nervous at first, wondering if I was about to hear a dark secret; he seemed so serious. We went down to the playroom, which is not necessarily private, especially with Tristan's deep resonating voice, but he didn't have a need for privacy. He just needed to share.

He told me about their group, about himself, and about Adam. It was the first time I learned the story behind "CWG" and that they had all been friends since middle school. He said

245

that a short time before Adam's death, they had developed a practice that Adam referred to as being "fake," isolating certain members, excluding, group texts and plans with one left off, etc. Adam refused to participate. He would leave the group and hang out with whoever they excluded and got angry at the rest. As it continued, Adam hung out with them less. The kids who were excluded were gone too. "Adam was the only true friend to all of us...he would always do the right thing."

Fortunately, before Adam died, they realized the negative impacts of their actions and started to change. Adam started hanging out again, and they had fun times. Tristan felt lucky about that, and grateful that the changes had occurred while he was still alive. Adam called him out as fake and he heard it. He decided to change, and Adam got to see it. When he died they were close friends again.

Most importantly, he shared that although Adam's passing was the hardest day of their lives, it changed everything for the whole group. This 16-year-old told me that Adam's death made them all realize the true meaning of "love and family" (his words). The one kid who had left the group before Adam died was pulled back in, a brother; and they all made a commitment to never be "fake" to each other again. They're sad Adam's gone, but his death was their wakeup, and his legacy, their reuniting and an unbreakable brotherly bond.

Tristan promised Adam to never be fake to anyone again, and he told me that day he knows that he can do it. He also shared something about Adam that he felt he didn't have the strength to imitate, the courage to call people out for being fake to others. Adam wasn't afraid to say, "That's messed up" or "You're being fake."

I think Tristan likely underestimated himself, and will, in fact, develop that strength. I'm pretty confident he already has.

#ForAdam

It's a cool morning as I type in the cottage in
Westhampton. I'm wearing a purple sweatshirt that says "New
Rochelle High School Football 2019 State Champions." My head
is restless, and I'm going to take a walk. If you happen to pass
me along my way to the ocean, you might stroll by and make
assumptions about what you see, about my life, about me in my
purple sweatshirt. You may suppose, "She must have a boy who
plays football, those football moms are crazy. I wonder if she
yells and has a blow horn (or worse, a flask) in her front hoodie
pocket?"

Or,

"Look at that, she's from New Rochelle, ground zero of
the Covid outbreak. I wonder if she had coronavirus, or knew
anyone that died."

You might wonder if I knew the original "index patient"
or lived within the confines of the "containment zone," that red-
dotted circle on the map, depicted in world news in the early
days of Covid as a restricted military zone, with prohibitions
from entering or leaving to contain the initial northeast breakout.
If you somehow get to know me, even peripherally or in a casual
expression of outreach, you might be surprised to discover that
though I live one block outside the red dots, I never saw a

soldier. The national guardsmen and women that arrived were kept busy sanitizing places of worship and handing out meals at schools that were closed by the edict.

Despite images on TV owing to the media's tendency to sensationalize, life was actually pretty normal in those first days in the "containment zone." Excepting prohibitions on gatherings of over 250 people (yes that's not a typo, in those earliest days "social distancing" was considered 250 or less), there was really nothing. In fact, when the circle was initially established, our own Mayor and County Executive, genuinely motivated to support businesses within its confines, did a photo op at a Chinese restaurant, urging citizens to come out and support local eateries and establishments. It was amazing how many texts I received from friends and family across the world inquiring how I was faring, whether I had the opportunity to stock up on supplies before the restrictions, and if it felt eerie not being able to come or go. Some of the texts came while I was at happy hour with friends in the containment zone (adhering to the mayor's urging). Admittedly, I was late getting dinner on the table that night, but it was the good company and half price enticements, not lines at military checkpoints or mandatory temperature checks that delayed me.

As we walk by one another, it definitely won't cross your mind that I do not have a son who plays football, but instead have one who is restricted from sports (football being the one he loved most) because of a heart condition that took the life of his little brother. You will likely not notice the small print that says, "#ForAdam." And even if owing to some powerfully keen visual perception you see it, you will not suspect the poignant and personal meaning of the hashtag for this lady passing. I might pass without either of us registering the other's presence, or one of us might imagine something interesting, incorrect, or not nice about the other. Either way, you will not fathom the depths of meaning connected to my sweatshirt.

Life isn't always as simple as what we see on TV or imagine from the snippets of people's lives we encounter. No judgement. When it comes to occasional intolerant assumptions based on incomplete information, I'm guilty; most of us are. Thanks to Adam, though, I'm more self-aware and work on it. It's a process.

New Rochelle High School Football provides a perfect example.

I was a multi-sport college athlete, so I can say from personal experience that female athletes get annoyed by football. Even if we are close to the individual athletes themselves, it is frustrating when they get so much attention and fanfare. Sometimes the football team is not even as good as the womens' programs, but they still get the money, the headlines, the better uniforms, more bling and fluff, and walk around campus like celebrities even in losing record seasons.

Many years after college, but before Adam died, I was a member of the Board of Education in New Rochelle. In our community, NRHS Football is big. They consistently have a strong team, with talented and dedicated coaches and a solid respected program. I'm chastened admitting that while I was on the board I fell into the group within the community who resented the attention directed at football over other sports programs, like cheerleading for instance, where we were national champions. I viewed NRHS Football as a privileged collective, not talented individuals who played the sport. (I didn't even know anyone that played.) I wasn't too impressed and had little interest or connection to any of the individuals involved.

My first experience of a reset, at being humbled in my superiority, was believe it or not, Ray Rice. Ray was a local kid who made it. He was a star running back at New Rochelle High School, went on to excel in college, made the NFL, and rose quickly to become a Pro Bowl Superstar for the Baltimore Ravens. In his stardom, he always remembered his roots and would return to New Rochelle for community events and impromptu appearances at practices and games to inspire the students.

Most people know that his successful career came to a sudden end after a terrible incident that was captured on video and went viral. It was very ugly. He hit a woman, his fiancé, hard, and it was caught on camera in all of it's disgusting, graphic, and despicable horror. His rise had been fast and furious; the crash was instant. He was banned, ostracized (some say scapegoated), and his career was over. No team would ever touch him. He was a pariah.

Just days after that horrible career-ending incident blew up the internet, New Rochelle High School had a home football game. The media were there because of the scandal. It brought attention not only to the former hometown hero but also our whole community. When the cameras showed up, where did they find the outcast at the center of the NFL drama? He was on the sidelines, next to his former coach. The weekend after it all broke, Ray Rice was right there on the field like nothing had ever happened.

As a school board member, I wondered how this could have been permitted. I was shocked anyone could have overlooked the implications, the message it sent to the players and to the community, the whole big picture. Other members of the Board of Education had the same questions. Suffice it to say, that in the discussion and answers, while I still regretted the attention and mixed messages it relayed for New Rochelle, I was left humbled by a coach who cared nothing about the things on which I was focused. My misperceptions of a boys' club culture were corrected as I witnessed behavior more typical of a committed family. My perceptions of a cocky coach and "protect our own" values were replaced by something more closely resembling a loyal loving father – like the dad in that parable of the prodigal son, who takes back and celebrates his ungrateful child after really bad behavior and his rock-bottom.

And Ray Rice? Well, my opinions and judgement about him were unchanged. It wasn't even about the person, this was good and evil, there was no gray area. If you saw it, you probably agree. There was nothing ambiguous, no window for excuses, and no forgiveness necessary. All the clarity I needed about him was right there in a 15-second clip all over the internet.

I didn't have any meaningful interaction or connections with NRHS football over the next few years, though my opinions and "meh" shifted slightly in a more positive direction. My kids were all into it and regulars at the games. Adam was my fifth child to attend NRHS. Over all those years, I didn't necessarily become a fan or gain much interest, but I liked seeing my family animated and excited in good seasons.

Four years after the Ray Rice scandal, and one year, almost to the day, after all the football players had prominently stood together at Adam's funeral, the team was once again on a road to the state championship. They would be playing in the state semifinal game. I was that much more interested now with an Adam connection, after learning what a fan he'd been.

It was the Friday afternoon before the game, a few days after the first anniversary of Adam's death (a few of the players had come to the house to pay respects). I was sitting alone in my kitchen recalling that same game one year before, just one day before he died. I remembered him getting ready to go, and waiting to be picked up by Johnny's friend Max to make the 2-hour trek up to Troy, NY for the exciting semifinal. The day was abnormally freezing with a predicted wind chill at game time below zero. He and I had argued over his choice of clothes. He'd refused to wear anything sensible and went off in his favorite, but really dumb for the weather, jean jacket. He had gotten it for his birthday months before; he loved that jacket and it was great on him. I vividly recalled my anxiety over how he would make it through a long game so inappropriately dressed (even refusing gloves).

Now, a year later, I teared up and shook my head at my ignorance. How stupid was my focus on something so minor in the oblivion of what would transpire the very next day. (I don't shake my head or tell myself I'm stupid anymore, but that first year, in my initial stages of darkness I was harder on myself.) As I sat there remembering, I felt moved to write and send the team good wishes, and a little bit of Adam, their biggest fan. It was weird how easily it came to me. I opened the computer, wrote and pushed send, as if it was from him through my fingers on the keyboard.

To: Coach Lou DiRienzo
From: Naomi Brickel
Date: Fri, Nov 16, 2018 at 5:11 PM
Subject: Good Luck

Hi Coach DiRienzo,

I wanted to wish you and the team good luck tomorrow. Last year my son, Adam, spent some of his final hours here on Earth freezing in his jean jacket cheering on the Huguenots in Troy. We were all energized over those weeks as your team pushed forward in the playoffs, and we were all sad at the outcome.

I will always remember feeling such warmth watching so many of the players on the team return the favor by attending his funeral. I was so proud of Adam that they knew him and wanted to be there ... and I was so proud of each of those players in how they represented themselves, their team, NRHS, and our community as a whole with such dignity and respect. It was an incredible comfort and gave me joy in a time of crushing sadness.

Recently, one of the players mentioned Adam's name in a social media post about this weekend's game. Someone showed it to Adam's little brother, Jude, and to say that made his day is an understatement. He was on cloud nine, feeling as if Adam was remembered by superstars. And I guess he was!

I will be keeping all of you in my prayers tomorrow, and I know Adam will be watching from his seat of honor up above. Please don't hesitate to ask him to pull some strings!! He had a way of reassuring everyone that everything was going to be ok. I would feel free to let him know that anything less than a state championship is simply not ok, so he better pull his weight!!

Many thanks to all of you for bringing our family Joy. Good luck!

Naomi Brickel, Adam's mom

~

Even in my email effort to show gratitude and send good wishes, I wrote to a collective group, a team. My letter was to a unit, not individual players who happened to share talent and affinity, each with their own separate lives and experiences, and individual friends of Adam's. I really didn't know or perceive any of them as persons, boys.

But two days later, after a big win, the connections started through texts:

To Mac Coughlin, NRHS Quarterback:

> *Hi Mac. This is Naomi Brickel. Adams mom. I got your number from Pat Swift. He shared two of your posts including the one about praying to Adam at halftime. I can't tell you how much it means to my family to have Adam remembered. These are probably the biggest moments thus far in the lives of you and your teammates. To know that Adam is accompanying you all gives us Hope and Joy. I only have your number but please thank all of your teammates for the shoutouts. Know that we are praying for you all and rooting you on. And it means so much to us (especially my sons Jude and JohnPaul) that you are carrying Adam with you! Good luck.*

Mrs. Brickel, no problem. I help coach Jude in lacrosse and I was good friends with both Adam and johnPaul as you would say. After having that email you wrote to us read by our coach, the whole team started crying and we realized that we were going to play for adam. At halftime when we were losing everyone seemed down, I started crying and prayed to Adam knowing he would deliver just like you said he would, so thank you for raising the kindest soul ever, and Thank you for giving us the power with that email to win that game.

~

Hello Mrs. Brickel, I am Matthew klein a
senior at NRHS. I am the schools varsity sports
photographer and have been traveling with the
football team all season. Yesterday prior to the
game in Middletown, the team came together in
one of the rooms and Coach Rhett spoke to us as
a team about what we mean to the school and
community. After he read the team the letter
you sent to Coach D. By the end of the letter
everyone in the room was emotional and crying
because they realized how they truly have a
impact in their community. When Coach Rhett
finished reading the letter and left the room the
team came together and decided that the ring
they are fighting for is not just for them. They
are bringing this home for the school,
community, and Adam. The team took the field
about a hour later with the motto #forAdam
knowing that they were not going down
without a fight and that they were not coming
home with "anything less than a state
championship". Though this week the team is
practicing and playing for Adam and the
community I felt as though you should be able
to see and hear Coach Rhett read this letter to
the team so attached is the video I took
yesterday before the game of him reading the
letter to the team. You can just imagine the
emotions in the room even though I do not
show it on camera. I am very sorry for your

255

loss. And want you to know that we as a school, community, and team are here for you and are going to make Adam proud. -Matthew Klein

~

Hello Mrs. Brickle, this is Corey Baron. I don't know if you remember me but I was at your house last Sunday evening. I play for the New Rochelle High School Football Team. I just wanted to say from me and on behalf of my teammates, we were very moved by the email you sent to our coach. When it was read to us, to say we were emotional is an understatement. I don't know if you're aware but we won yesterday and are now going to play for a State Championship. I wanted to let you know that we couldn't have done it without Adam looking out for us from above like he always does. We are beyond thankful to have you and your family cheering us on. THANK YOU !

~

Thank you Ms. Brickel!! Your letter had our entire team very emotional yesterday and it got us going before the game. This is Halim Dixon-King #7 🖤

~

I just wanna thank you for the letter you wrote yesterday for the team

It was very emotional much love 🖤

Not to Spoil the Ending... but everything is going to be ok

Thank you so much. Who is this?

I'm Ali Paul number 20 on varsity

Thank you Ali. Did you know Adam?

Yea he was a great friend of mine

Since middle school

That makes me feel so happy. Thank you for keeping his memory alive and for letting him accompany you in this incredible time

We gonna win it all for him !!

You are making me cry. Actually I was already crying. Thank you!

🖤

And so many others, Instagram posts, Snapchats, calling out Adam with the "#ForAdam". Now, for me, this football team, this victorious, amazing, winning team, became individuals: players, boys, other mother's sons, each a "divine spark" showering his light on me through texts and hashtags.

~

They were "going to the Dome," the Syracuse University Carrier Dome, to the NY State Championship! The days leading up were electric. Everything focused on this team; and as the players prepared, and rallied with the community, the "#ForAdam" was everywhere: posts, tweets, videos, snaps, stories, etc. Adam was in the middle of it all, like a star player, so prominently a part. It took on such momentum both in our home and in the community that Jude and I decided to make the trek to Syracuse. We drove up with my friend Jeffrey, who arranged the invitation for us to be on the sidelines for the game, and even in the locker room. There in the intensity of the locker room before a state championship game was where I learned the most about this team, valuable lessons about collective and individual lives and my own perceptions, and, for the first time, about another side of Ray Rice.

Ray had been helping out with the team since that day years ago when, in his lowest moment, his coach took him back, and stood next to him on the sidelines. I don't know if he was a coach in a formal capacity. I really don't know any of the details, all I saw was his love for the game, his coach, and those boys, as well as the reciprocation. For this game, the biggest game in any of their lives, Ray would do the pregame "talk" and Jude and I were blessed to witness it. The hair on my arms stood up the whole time. I had tears in my eyes. Jude was hypnotized. The players, accustomed to his inspiration, listened, serious and reverent. It was inspiring to behold, a highly trained, diverse brigade, mature, self-disciplined, serious, loving and dedicated to one another. They were young men of dignity and character.

One might picture a coach before the biggest game firing up the team with testosterone-induced, warrior-like rally cries. But it wasn't that at all. He spoke to them about representing their community, and each player's own individual dignity. I don't recall the words, just that it was nothing I would have ever expected for a pregame pep talk, no stereotypical mention of war or domination. Rather, this inspired man, the same Ray Rice upon whom I had formulated a blanket judgement based on seconds of his life, appealed to each of those players' individual worthiness, love, self-respect, and respect for the community – their own individual divine sparks and those of the people who looked up to them – to inspire and motivate their best performance. As I stood there watching and listening, I found myself wishing that my young son standing next to me could have a coach or mentor like the man in front of me, someone to emulate like him. I stood there wishing my child, like these boys, had someone like this in his life, an example of what a man should be. ...

... Well, maybe... that is, if it wasn't the guy in the video, I second guessed.

~

The energy in the locker room was intense. I couldn't believe that we had this opportunity to be such an intimate part of it. I understood why as the team prepared to rush the field. As each player got up, put on his helmet, one by one, just like the kids had all done the night of the visitation at my house, each came and stood right in front of me. Some took a deep breath, each hugged and/or touched me as they passed. Some cried (I certainly did), some blessed themselves, many whispered to me, "For Adam." I got a fat lip from all the shoulder pads in the strong embraces. NRHS football players are a poignant bunch.

Sadly, the winner of the NYS 2018 Football Championship was Aquinas, a school from upstate. We could point to bad calls, compare our local public school to a school that recruited from all over the state, but in the end the trophy was not coming back to NewRo. We lost and it was a such a blow. In the locker room after, the tears were profuse. I got a chance to speak and thank them all. I gave each one the card we had made for the funeral, with Adam's picture, the quote from Dr. Seuss reminding not to be sad it's over, but happy it happened, and the quote from St. Paul about the Spirit inside. It just so happened that there had been 50 left over, enough for each person there. I was able to remind them of Adam's words, "Everything is going to be ok," and I thanked them for the incredible gift they had given our family. I knew that Jude and I were now a part of theirs.

The first half hour of the ride back Jude could not speak in his sadness. My friend Jeffrey and I did not try to cheer him, but rather, just let him experience it. It was the most tears I had seen from him since Adam's death. He tended to keep it bottled up, to the point that I worried. I'm not sure when his tears ended and the sleep overcame him, but I knew both were healthy and important. He slept almost the whole 5-hour ride home.

~

A year later, November 2019, Huguenot Football was on another run, dedicated again to Adam in what would have been his senior year. They lost their beloved head coach in the middle of it all. However, despite ugly politics, a media spotlight, and adults behaving badly around them, a group of individual champion football players, boys, remained focused and disciplined as a team. Their championship game ended up being rescheduled for a day earlier to beat out an impending blizzard, and they were rushed onto busses to arrive in time at the stadium. Everything was against them.

But a week later I was wearing my new "NRHS 2019 State Champions" sweatshirt.

~

For me, in many ways, the team's "#ForAdam" seemed as much from him, with accompanying gifts and lights only he could have shared. I have learned a lot from Adam about seeing past the collective, past the group identification or label – whether it's the initials after a name, the car, clothing styles, religion or skin color – to the actual person and their unique "divine spark." Knowing more about Adam's connections with some who got missed in the shadows, and all of those individual players who considered him a close cherished friend, who shared how he helped them or was kind, provides important lessons:

-First, not to get so wrapped up in my own stuff that I miss others.

-Not to get stuck on the surface, or categorize.

-Stay connected to what is real, not what people tell you to think.

-"Don't be fake!"

-And all that I've learned from the transformation of my perceptions of a "football program" to individual players, persons who came to a funeral, boys who sent texts, individual human hugs on the way out to the championship field – the gift to perceive each person, just like Adam did.

Adam was onto something the way he noticed stuff and the actual persons that most of us might miss. In the polarization that defines our times, maybe we all need to try to look deeper, beyond the surface of that celebrity on TV, the kid who looks different or up to no good on the corner, the cop, the person in the fancy car, the person in the dumpy car, the politician on the wrong side, the unusual religious practice, or just my purple sweatshirt. Maybe we just all need to make more of an effort to stop at the quick superficial judgement, to look the complex human life behind the facade, even beyond the CNN or Fox filter (whichever side you're on) to which we typically limit our awareness. Is it possible for us to maintain the humility to admit that behind the seemingly unforgivable opinion or behavior of that "other," there is a real person, someone who likely had a mom that loved him, or a child he loves, that he or she smiles, laughs and even cries like us? Perhaps by pushing ourselves to see deeper, these dark times we commiserate might be lit up brightly by innumerous "divine sparks" of those we encounter but typically fail to notice every single day.

Here's how Adam drove this home for me.

A few months after the championship celebrations, "Coach D" was being honored. He was to be inducted into the Westchester County Athletics Hall of Fame, along with my own high school coach, Cathi Wasilik. I was excited to attend, for both of them. During the cocktail hour, my friend Gina, a football mom with a blow horn like the one I described at the beginning of this chapter, came over and hugged me in the huge wonderful way she does.

"Hey, I need you to talk to Ray. He has some ideas that I told him you'd be good to help with. Hey Ray, come here."

We talked. He was looking for ways to get help for players who lacked support to navigate the college admissions process. Sure, I would help. Not long after, I reached out to him about a couple of young men I'm close to who needed some support and mentoring. He jumped at the opportunity to help in return.

Ray and I have discovered a shared goal of making our community better, and even new initiatives we plan to take on together. In the process, I've learned a lot more about Ray Rice too. I have seen him with his wife, Janay (the same woman in the video) and his beautiful kids. I've learned about his personal journey after the incident, including working with the NFL efforts to address domestic violence, about his assuming credible ownership and accountability for those horrible actions, and even his own necessary transformation and healing. Most of all, I've witnessed an unexpected and inspiring humility and charity.

If someday you happen to see Ray and I walking down the street, judging solely by our outward appearances (unless of course we're both wearing our purple sweatshirts), you will likely assume we don't even know each another. Even people who know me will find this part of my life surprising, and I think people in Ray's life might find his friendship with this 50-something white lady with six kids a bit curious too. In fact, we have much more in common than a connection with New Rochelle football, or even some special young men we care about. Still, no one would suspect the reality of the depth of our friendship, or that when we are together how deep and intense our conversations go, often to tears. We appear very different on the outside, but in our connection, we have discovered that we are much more alike than our individual surface appearances suggest.

Incredibly, we've discovered something crazy yet profound that we share in common: the awareness that the worst thing that ever happened to each of us was also be the best thing that ever happened, setting us each on our own new course, towards the discovery of what is real and important and to the deep resonating joy we have found right within ourselves – and now each other.

Adam took me on a journey of self-discovery through Ray Rice – past the person I first conceived in my head from 15 seconds on the internet, or even the better version in the locker room or the mentor I text for a kid who needs a good, caring man in his life, and friend who texts me to help one of his players. Yes, Adam taught me to see, enabling me to know and experience a father and husband I would feel very proud of if he were my own son, or even married to my daughter. Like every person, Ray Rice is much more complex than what I initially concluded from a few seconds of his life – and definitely redeemable. In fact, for me he is one of Adam's most wonderful gifts. ... *#FromAdam*

#YUTIGHT?

Adam, whenever things weren't going well you noticed right away. Thank you for always being the positive one, the one who always cheered me up. You were so happy and always looked at the good of everything... You left us with positive thoughts 24/7...
Love Saba R. 🖤

I knew your son. I loved him very much and he was very dear to my heart.... Words can't explain how happy he was and how many times he made me happy.... I can't even explain how he made me feel on the days when I was sad... Mitchelle O.

Adam was loved by so many people. As long as we never forget him, it will be like nothing happened. It will hurt us at certain times. But it will be okay. Love, Ella K.

Yes, you are right, Ella

And, not to spoil the ending ...

... but everything's going to be ok...

Dreams

Occasionally I heard indirectly about another friend's dream, or their child's. I would ask the messenger to please relay that I would love to hear it, but never heard anything more. One family I went to directly was the Floods. I heard that a few of them had dreams of Adam, and I felt close and comfortable enough to reach out. I've known the Dad, Rob, since second grade. We went to elementary school together and live in the same neighborhood. I'm friends with his wife, Cathy, and their boys are all close to Johnny and Adam's age and were friends too. Some of them had experienced dreams with Adam, simple, most just a smile or wave, or his company and a sense of peace. I wonder what made him choose their family. I am happy they enjoyed his presence and appreciate that I got to learn of it.

They were the only ones I went to. I heard about others who never shared. I must admit, that while I understand how difficult it would be to reach out, it was painful to know he was out there, connecting with people and I was left out. It was like there were pieces of him, treasures, that were falling through my fingertips. People wanted to help, I had meals for months, and that remains so appreciated, but I would have given up the convenience of not cooking every one of those meals for just one dream, that thread of his presence, that I didn't hear. I know it's complicated. Everyone responds to emotional situations (like the relaying of an intimate dream with someone else's dead child, duh?) differently, which creates uncertainty. While I might crave every detail of your dream; another mother may find it too painful. The one thing nobody wants is to lay more pain on a grieving parent. One might also be reluctant to intrude on the family's privacy. All legitimate considerations.

But for the potential gift that your dream or story could be to a family, I think some amount of risk and vulnerability is warranted. Here's my advice if you ever find yourself in a similar situation: reach out, pick up the phone, text, or email. Make the reason for your outreach indirect, and start by telling the person that you've been thinking about them and want to let them know. You can offer assistance if they ever need it. Then understatedly mention it. "I had a dream," or "I have a story about 'blank' I'm happy to share it with you if you'd like. Let me know. ..." If you have an Adam story or a dream that I haven't heard, it's not too late. Please share, they're my treasures.

Adam's friend Tristan came to me with his. Tristan wanted to tell me his experiences with Adam, including his frequent dreams. Admittedly, I was a bit jealous, but more excited for him to share. I felt dreams were the only way Adam could stay connected and communicate messages. Most of Tristan's dreams were just an awareness of his presence, Adam being there among a group or in a situation, always lending a peaceful aura. But there was one that was more detailed, where Adam came to him and they hugged each other. Tristan asked, "When are you ever coming back? We miss you so much. We need you here with us." Adam just smiled, and said, "Everything will be ok. I promise." Then left.

I remembered the words that the boy in Adam's chemistry class had attributed to Adam just days before he died, when Adam had walked across a classroom to an upperclassman he barely knew, whose sadness he had noticed from across the room. It was the story I had shared in my speech at their graduation. "Everything is going to be ok, man, I promise." When Tristan told me this dream, the hair stood up on my arms, my eyes filled, and I hugged him. I was so grateful for that treasure, Adam's important message that kept coming through.

Almost exactly a year later, the weekend before the second anniversary, I had my own related dream, although Adam was not actually in it. It was a dream about Tristan. We were planning to commemorate the anniversary a day early, as it was Veterans Day and school was closed. (It is not surprising that Adam ensured a day off from school.) The Sunday night before we would have another chili and grilled cheese dinner and the friends and neighbors would come again. There would be another mass, and then back to the house for bagels. Basically, a repeat of the first year.

I had the dream Saturday morning; it was about what would happen in the coming days, a "bagels at the house after" dream. His friends were there, and Tristan called me over to show me something. He was pointing to a wood plaque on the shelf in my kitchen that says,

"Not to spoil the ending, but everything is going to be ok."

I bought the plaque many years before Adam died. I was in DC for work with Yvette, my friend and colleague, and we were window shopping in Georgetown. I saw the plaque in a gift shop, and its message resonated. At the time Kit was a junior in high school. Junior year is a stressful year when you are a serious student, as she was. She had many AP classes, was worried about college, experienced the typical high school stresses, etc. I liked the carefree sentiment as a reminder for both me and Kit not to take life's everyday issues so seriously. It would be good to have it hanging in our kitchen and it did for many years.

Now in my dream, Tristan was excited, he pointed at the plaque and said, "Look at this! It's what Adam always tells me in my dreams!"

The plaque had been there forever, and I had stopped noticing, and never made the connection.

"Everything is going to be ok. I promise."

OK, Adam, now I really get it.

The plaque is more important now too, and I notice it. Adam was right all along, not only his messages in dreams after his death, but in how he noticed and approached those who needed to hear the same while he was alive. In my speech at the graduation, I did not share the end of the story, but it's important. When the boy from Chemistry class stood up at the candle service that day to share his story about Adam coming over to him, he finished with tears in his eyes, and a poignant question. "Adam's gone. Who's going to tell me it's ok now?"

Maybe in that question we discover a thread of Adam's purpose, and perhaps even a mission for each one of us.

Washable Paint

Halloween was two weeks before Adam died. Johnny and some friends had party plans the weekend before, which (of course) entailed bloody costumes and (of course) spray paint. I don't know what it is with the Xy chromosome and spray paint and graffiti. My boys have always had affinities for both. I recall a prolonged period when the youngest (it was either Jude or Adam) were little enough to still have a limited vocabulary, yet a common excited scream in the car being, "Look Mom! Graffiti!!" Years before a regional "artist" left his signature watermelon slice all over Westchester, and at the time, JohnPaul had been obsessed by the sightings. For Johnny and the watermelons, I think it was the combination of 'difficult to get to' locations and the creativity. He has an eye and appreciation for design, and is very physically daring. He's gone through phases in both clothing and residential design, likes to draw, can actually sew, works with architecture software, does backflips when he cliff dives, and once climbed out a third story window during a nor'easter. For Jude or Adam (it would be the same for either) the two or three-year-old fascination was likely admiration for the nerve and rebelliousness it takes to spray-paint on public property.

This particular Saturday, Johnny had three or four friends over with old clothes and a can of red spray paint. A recipe for disaster, yes, it probably crossed my mind. Sometimes though, especially on a Saturday after my week at work and running a house of eight, ready for a break myself, I might be prone to mother in a 'path of least resistance' style. This particular Saturday afternoon that path was not a trip to the garage with the appropriate command, "Boys! No!" but a pop out to meet a friend for lunch and afternoon drinks. Their creativity progressed undisturbed.

The Monday morning after was actually Halloween, but the weekend's paint and parties were over. Adam took an early morning lifeguarding class at school. I drove him those mornings on the way to work. I have a habit of always beating my kids to the car. Go figure. I am a bit type A, with an internal clock that runs three minutes early. Contrasted by my teenage boys' clocks that tend to run behind, or are just broken, I found myself that Monday sitting in the front seat waiting for Adam. I was startled as I got in and turned on the car by loud, blaring, abrasive, explicit rap music, owing to the different tastes and volume levels my boys enjoyed. One of them had borrowed my car and disconnected my phone to put theirs in. I turned it all off and connected my phone to the car electronic system, and, with all resituated, took a relaxing breath, leaving behind all of this associated chaos of early Monday morning departure. I was just looking out the front window as Adam got into the car, but instead of being welcomed by Mom Zen, he was greeted with an instinctually blurted out, "WTF!" (spelled out).

There is a sizable boulder at the end of our driveway, large enough that you can't move it. It's a big smooth rock, offering a natural complement to a grass and firepit area surrounded by untamed forsythia bushes, right when you pull in our driveway. It's a lovely setting, a first welcoming introduction to our home and pleasant family life there. There on the rock, in red spray paint, in a horrible wild and messy graffiti-like font (if you can refer to such gross defacement in standard terms like "font") it said, "JUDE."

Adam, alarmed by my outburst, asked me what was wrong.

I screamed, "Look!!!!" and motioned to it.

Unfazed, he calmly responded, "Mom, jeeeeeze, relax! Washable paint."

"Oh my God, really??" I had never heard of washable paint, but it made more sense now, how the boys had so liberally used it on their clothes and each other.

"Yes! Maaaan! You need to relax!"

"Oh, phew. Thank God!" We drove to school calmly. I went on with my day. Washable paint. He was right. I needed to chill. Why did I let myself get worked up so easily? Washable paint.

I never noticed the "JUDE" in blood-like red spray paint graffiti on that large rock at the end of my driveway as I pulled in each day over the next several weeks. Since it would go away, it was already off my mind. Of course, something a lot worse than graffiti-stupidity would soon transpire. Two weeks later, Adam was dead and people started showing up. JohnPaul's spray paint buddies were the ones who came as we arrived back home from the hospital. I remember walking into Johnny's room that morning to check on him and seeing them all asleep on the floor, those same stupid boys. Those same beautiful, loyal, brave, dumb boys.

It wasn't until a few weeks after Adam died that I found myself in the car one morning, on my way to work, looking out at the rock.

"JUDE"

It was still there, as bright and ugly as that first Monday morning. But it had certainly rained since then ... Washable paint...

Have you ever heard of washable paint? Google it. It actually does exist. You'll find images of plastic bottles labeled "Crayola" that look suitable for art or kindergarten classrooms. It does not come in acrylic or oil-based formulas, or spray paint cans. Washable paint. He was full of sh--. Adam always hated seeing me tense. All my boys do. They will all tell me whatever they think I need to hear rather than the truth if it is upsetting, and it annoys me immensely. Now I was laughing out loud. I felt his laughter and his love in that moment, and I became aware of the humble love, that chaotic Monday morning, in his relaxed, instinctual, "washable paint" response.

Some of the signs that Adam has sent me since his death have to do with the loneliness I have endured these last years. They've included a "someone, someday" and have come through in my most forsaken and despondent moments.

In one instance, I was asleep in the cottage in Westhampton. I had fallen asleep just 40 or so minutes earlier, and I was woken by his voice. It was in my head and not out loud, but it was distinct, almost palpable (or something like that). After, I remembered the sound of his voice and his words. He shared details about someone who would be there eventually for me, and ended with, "but you'll just have to wait." It made sense, Doug is still alive, even if he's mostly gone mentally and physically. I plan to finish it out like people who promise their lives to each other do. But Adam assured me it would be ok. I was comforted, hopeful, and less lonely, even as my actual situation, levels of responsibility, and solitary sadness remained unchanged.

Another time, I was alone in the dining room doing paperwork, feeling overwhelmed by insurance refusals, bills, and complex stuff that I needed to figure out (in addition to the laundry, tidying, meals, and that whole job thing). This particular day it all felt crushing. I was losing hope that I could handle it all. Doug was never coming home. I wished I had a partner to carry some of the pain, shoulder some of the responsibility, or just hold me. Once again I felt so alone. My eyes filled with tears. I moaned, sobbed, then I screamed. Suddenly, the wood plaque on the kitchen shelf fell spontaneously, the same one from my dream.

"Not to spoil the ending, but everything is going to be ok."

It was literally on a shelf, there were no windows open, no breeze. Unprompted, it fell over, off the shelf to the floor, and crashed with a loud bang, startling me and redirecting my self-pity to action. I jumped up to get it. (That plaque is so important to me now, with its words and the associated dreams and stories.) I picked it up. It wasn't broken. It was fine. I felt Adam chuckle, and even felt him say, *"Mom, really, RELAX?! What have I told you?"* Distracted from my angst and sadness, I chuckled too, and put it back on the shelf. It had never fallen unprompted before and has not since. I went back to the bills, less alone.

These signs came deliberately, so overtly, that I never even questioned his presence making it happen. They distracted me from my sadness each time, and I hang onto them to carry me through subsequent dark periods. In those horrible desolate moments, he's comforted, calmed, and fortified my strength with a reassurance that it's all going to be ok, that I won't always be - that I'm not - alone. Whether his assurances about someone in my future are true or not remains to be seen. Either way, they did the trick in the moment, and got me through. And now I've discovered a peace and joy within my own self that I never experienced before. So, I'm not really lonely anymore anyway.

Were his signs simply "washable paint?" Something to distract me, carry me through, a white lie or game of semantics? *"I said 'lonely' not 'alone', mom."* It doesn't matter I guess, either way it worked its purpose. And, if so, thanks Adam - I guess. It's reassuring, somehow, to know death has not changed anything...

"Mom! Why you so tight?!... everything is going to be ok, I promise!"

And he's right.

Apartments, College, Butterflies, Japan

I can't begin to detail the trials we experienced as a family in the weeks and months after Adam's death. We were all under one roof, processing our grief in our own ways, individually but on top of each other, with Doug's illness progressively worsening. It was hard to not be angry, both at God and each other. Bickering, frustration, grief, clutter, mess - all of it would have been tough in the best of circumstances. Understandably, there was very little positive that any of us could see or even notice. The house was too crowded, but it didn't feel like the time to be encouraging kids to leave the nest. And yet, it was exactly what they - and we - all needed.

It was almost 8 months after, June, and Mindy would be graduating from New Rochelle High School, a huge accomplishment six years in the making. Because of her disabilities she had not followed the typical four-year progression for a high school student. But here she was at the point of completion, graduating with a real high school diploma, having met all of the necessary credit and testing requirements. It was certainly something to be proud of and celebrate, and we did our best. Even more noteworthy, though, was the fact that immediately following graduation, the very next day, she would be traveling to Japan to compete internationally with her highly acclaimed NRHS Chorale. This was truly an amazing culmination, so much to be proud of ... I was a nervous wreck.

How would my vulnerable child with autism and other disabilities last through a 25-hour flight? Who would help her pick out the right clothes for the performances? How would the other kids treat her? Would she be excluded or teased? Who would room with her? How could she possibly figure out how to spend and budget the money I sent her with? What would happen if she lost her passport or phone? What if she had a seizure?

I barely remember her graduation at all, distracted about the next day. Mindy was nervous, agitated and difficult to live with the week leading up to her departure, and so was I. Japan! Of all the places to select for this year's trip! She kept reminding me that though several of her siblings had traveled alone to Spain, this was the furthest any Brickel had ever traveled in the world. Yes, yes, yes, I knew that! I didn't need the frequent reminders.

The departing flight was late at night and we would spend the long day packing, go for a nice cheeseburger dinner (her favorite), and then to the airport. It was not enough to fill the long, slow, angst-filled day of waiting. On the way there we were distracted from our nerves-imposed shortness with each other by "almost fourth of July" fireworks. I took deep breaths and kept reassuring myself that I could do this, I only had to maintain my composure until I dropped her off, and once I pulled away I could cry.

And that's what happened. I dropped her with the group at the airport curb. I got out for a wonderful picture of her big smile with her closest friend and her noble teacher. We hugged, and I told her she was a rock star, that I was so proud, and that she was going to be great - trying to convince us both of the last part. I pulled away, about 100 yards further I pulled back over to pull up the maps on my phone, and couldn't help but burst out in tears. I wept, and looking up to our official Brickel Angel in Heaven, I made a strong, serious, and firm executive command.

"Don't you leave her side; do you understand me???"

~

Almost two weeks later, I was in the same spot, driving away from the airport again, this time with Mindy in the front seat next to me after an incredible trip (with daily Facetime updates keeping my anxiety at bay). She's not much of a talker and I had anticipated that she would not be forthcoming in the car with details and stories I was dying to hear. I was calculated in planning for this. I gave her a few minutes to just be happy and quiet in the front seat. Then I offered the following first stab at a negotiation for conversation.

"Ok, so I promise I won't ask you a lot of questions, and I'll even let you not even talk for the rest of the ride, if you agree to just tell me one great thing that happened this week and one thing that was not so great. Deal?"

"Ugh. Fine. There was a real live Mario Cart driving around.... Oh, and there were deer that bowed..." it went on a bit with several stories and details, a pleasant surprise ... and then, "Oh, and Mom, there was this weirdest thing that happened. There was this place where you remember lost souls, and we did this candle thing, so of course... well you know. I don't mean to upset you. Ok, I mean I know he's dead and all but I felt like Adam was with me. Like not really there, but like I kept feeling like he was next to me, like not really next to me, but it was like he was not dead and was in Japan with me. I even felt like I could hear him laughing..."

Holy sh-- ...

~

JohnPaul was the first to express a need to get out of the sad darkness that our home had become. It was late in the summer, but we found an opportunity in Maine where he would be able to enter a building certification program at a community college. It happened quickly, almost too quickly, without the months of planning and research I preferred to put into things. He would leave suddenly the day after Adam's 16th birthday. He needed to get away, pull his life together, forge a direction, and he was ready. I was agitated, stressed, and felt a sense of guilt and insecurity. Was this the right thing? Was it too soon? Was he too vulnerable to be so far? The mother in me was not done protecting after his incredible trauma.

My friend, Nancy, drove us up there. We would have a nice lunch in Kennebunkport and make a fun day of it. That was how she fixed everything, fun was always the excuse she gave for her assistance. We left in the middle of the night and arrived at the house - a house of strangers - where JohnPaul would live for the next nine months. The others stared at the new arrival, it felt lonely and far. We went out to lunch, and Nancy conveniently left us together while she met a friend. Johnny expressed to me that it would be hard, but it was right. He needed this fresh start. We went back to the house where I quickly hugged him and left. As I walked out I saw a woman talking to a young man very seriously, a tattoo-covered woman, the house "supervision" - she didn't even look up. "Who was I leaving my precious son with?" I wondered and second-guessed. Since she didn't look back, I was able to look more closely and noticed the tattoos on her neck were butterflies.

Butterflies had taken on symbolism for me and others as an "Adam sign." As we drove away, I was sad, but comforted; and though the tattoos might have remained slightly unnerving, they prompted the awareness that I wasn't leaving him alone at all. He had an angel there with him, Adam. What I didn't know yet was that I had actually left him with two angels, or of the beautiful loving relationship that would transpire between Johnny and Laura, the woman with butterfly tattoos. She would play such a loving and important role in his new life and direction. Laura and I became close over calls checking on him and still keep in touch. Frequently, I have started to share something about Adam and instead promised to write it down and send in an email. Those emails never got sent but became the stories that initiated this manuscript. ... Laura, thank you for standing in at the most critical time and for inspiring me to sit down to write.

~

Kit was also ready for a fresh start. We were struggling to maintain our peace, and though the decision for her to look for a new place first arose out of tension, I will always joyfully remember her excitement when she told me about the apartment she had found. It seemed like a great deal, a perfect location in Hoboken, NJ, with easy access to the PATH train which stopped across the street from her job in NYC. It was almost too good to be true and we were filled with anticipation as it all fell into place - and it did!

Nancy again played an important accompanying role, offering to help with the move. She agreed to drive and gathered essentials for Kit in her new place. Her presence kept the mood light during what would have otherwise been a stressful and emotion-filled afternoon. Again, I second-guessed whether this was right or too soon. Was she still too pained and vulnerable? All of the feelings I had with Johnny on repeat.

We parked and unloaded, met one of her new roommates, and set up her room. We ran out to the store to stock up the fridge and pantry. Things like a big shopping are harder in the city, just to find parking to unload. We had too many bags and not enough arms, and walked up to the locked outside door. As Kit began to dig for her new key, a young man came up with his own key out. He lived in the apartment upstairs, and offered to assist. He explained the trash detail. Besides being adorable, there was something about him that gave me peace, maybe it was the idea of an apartment full of protective guys above, or his unassuming gentle manner.

"Thanks so much for all your help. And this is Kit, she'll be on the second floor. What's your name?" I asked.

"No problem. You're welcome. Nice to meet you all. Welcome. I'm Adam."

Ok. I guess this was the right thing. Nancy and I drove away in tears.

~

The house would continue to become even lighter. It wasn't long before Billy was ready to be out from under my motherly reminders to turn off lights, throw away beer cans, pick up his clothes, hang up towels, and keep the weed out of the house. He found a very affordable room in a house in Mt. Vernon. The rent had to be paid in cash, but it had no lease, and it was on a train line!

"Mt. Vernon West?" I asked, hoping for the "nicer" side of the city.

"No, even better. It's on our line, Mt. Vernon East!"

My heart sunk slightly into my gut. It wasn't the best area. Having approached life similarly at his age, I knew that like most young people, he likely didn't possess an appropriate sense of his mortality, awareness of his safety - or lack thereof. I decided it was not in my control anyway, and I needed to put him under his brother's heavenly care. Immediately, I was reassured that our angel up above was on call when Billy sent me a screenshot of the map of his new place. His house was on a main road, at the intersection where Adams Place turns into Martens Blvd.

Yes, Adam Martin Brickel, it's all going to be ok. Thank you. I get it!

P.S. I Love You

August 17, 2020

It's 2020, and we're in tough times. Six months ago, Covid shut down the whole planet. Life in the 21st century halted for what we initially, naively, hoped would be two weeks. Months later there is no end in sight, only a clear awareness that some things will never be the same. Kids will be starting school shortly, "learning" on the devices parents were previously warned to limit or prohibit, from their beds or kitchen tables, not classrooms. Many still haven't left their homes. Others speak about losing motivation at work, feeling flat, or being depressed. "Covid crazy" is a term that became part of the lexicon among my friends. People are lonely, struggling to motivate themselves to face days lacking human connection, further separated by the way they choose to respond to the pandemic, daunted by the winter and unknowns ahead. Whether you are the "bubble" family who left your groceries on the steps to decontaminate, or the one whose kids were having parties in the basement, biking with friends, and going to the store without gloves, you likely perceive the other as lacking reasoned judgement.

Quite frankly, even as hope increases in a vaccine, things don't feel lighter. Our culture is isolated beyond Covid through self-selected divisions. It's cliché to refer to the polarization in our society, being so present and obvious, but the increase over the past several years is frightening. Riots and burning cities were regular clips on TV and the internet this summer. Conversations about timely issues are adversarial, emotion-fueled, and defensive. Political discourse has been reduced to visceral reactions to others opinions who either support or hate Trump. Whichever side you're on, "truth" and "facts" are what's on your personalized social media feeds, or the TV channels you watch. The other side (whichever it is) is obviously and willfully criminal, irresponsible, liars, morally bankrupt, or hate-filled.

My personal life circumstances are no picnic either. In addition to processing the still recent death of Adam, I'm essentially a single parent struggling to raise a family and maintain a home in Westchester County, NY on a non-profit salary. State and federal budgets that fund my work are at risk due to economic uncertainty. My sick husband has been battling the progression of Parkinson's for the past nine years. He lives in a nursing facility that was shut down to visitors (including his wife and kids). He got Covid, associated delirium, and broke his hip, twice. He is still recovering from the second hip surgery due to a more recent fall, but his mind isn't. Because of the injury he was hospitalized, and I was able to visit and touch him for the first time in six months. I said goodbye when I left him, just in case. I live with a teenager and 20-somethings (enough said). Recently an accident with a plate hurled by his friend brought me to the ER with my youngest child, resulting in 13 staples in his head, and my daughter with autism and an intellectual disability had a seizure this week. Long before any of the details

I've articulated above ever occurred, a friend once joked that my life was like Job's.

It's Adam's birthday. He would have been 18 years old. His birthday had surrounding traditions in his life. And in his death, I have tried to keep them up. He and his sister, Kit, have summer birthdays exactly a week apart. Most years while Adam was alive, their birthdays fell over the two weeks that I took my work vacation. We spent most of that time in Westhampton, and would celebrate their birthdays together on the weekend that fell in between. Many of my siblings and their families would be around too. Dinners and cake with so many cousins, aunts, and uncles made it festive.

Vacations in late August inevitably come with a cold or rainy day or two, and there was a tradition for that too. This one became Adam's own special birthday thing because it was his favorite, a drive to the North Fork with a stop at The Love Lane Sweet Shoppe in Mattituck. One of the most frequent Adam questions during the month of August was, "When are we gonna go to Love Lane?" He loved this stop. We all did. We would spend time walking slowly around the small store, admiring the selection of gifts and novelties, as well as local North Fork t-shirts and paraphernalia. Each of us got our own bag that we filled with our individual personally selected assortment of old favorite, vintage, loose candies and gourmet chocolates. What was not to like? Adam insisted we do this for his birthday every year.

Some years, after the candy store we might stop at a winery traveling east along Route 25A. Doug and I had spent our honeymoon and most anniversaries enjoying Long Island's East End, and had a few favorite stops. We might continue our journey all the way to Orient Point, right to the tip of the island, where the ferry went to New London, CT. There were two years we actually took the ferry across to visit friends from our neighborhood at their summer place in Quonnie on the Rhode Island coast. The ferry was a fun adventure.

Most years we simply let the kids get out and walk on the smooth pebbled beach, watch the huge ferries come and go, and if it was hot, take a quick dip. Then we would head back, make the mandatory stop for oysters from a roadside farm stand in Oyster Ponds (I am a huge oyster fan and Doug was an expert shucker), and proceed to Greenport, a fun, bustling, summer town. There was always a stop there, either for lunch or ice cream, and a ride on the Carousel. In my memory, it is always Adam who got the golden ring!

We generally got home right before dinner, the perfect time for oysters and a glass of wine from the bottle we bought at whatever winery we had visited that day. The wine never seemed to be quite as good as it had tasted at the winery, in a beautiful setting with our kids running around. Either way, it paired well with the oysters, as the perfect end to perfect days.

Those are my favorite family memories; and the tradition is one I cherish. So, each year around Adam's birthday, I do all or part of it. Last year my friend Emily, who was visiting from Kentucky, joined me for it. In addition to bulk candy and wonderful chocolates, the Sweet Shoppe also carries little gifts and t-shirts. I decided to buy a gift for myself from Adam and picked out a nice faded "Love Lane" t-shirt. I got one for Kit too, seeing it as a way of celebrating their birthdays together.

As I continued to peruse, I noticed some shiny bracelets with little sayings on them. They jumped out at me because they were so bright, so I read each one. I was struck by one that read, "You Are My Sunshine." With all of Adams' connections and messages, it seemed his way of outreach, like he had put it there for me. The boy who came to me in the sun at his funeral, and the boy who then reminded me that my own soul's shine is even better than sunshine. Here was a wonderful cute shiny message (Adam loved bling) letting me know he was there. I bought it and loved it! There was no doubt that it came from him, and I cherished it. But a few days later as Emily left, something also told me that Adam would like her to have it - perhaps his gratitude for her enabling him to stay a part of me through the tattooed ashes she had arranged. I handed it over, a difficult decision but no remorse. It seemed right and fitting, and I never had any regrets about it at all.

That is, until this August, almost a year later. It was Adam's birthday month and I started to miss the bracelet. In a strange, real, and yet still no-remorse way I wished I had it back on my wrist. (Perhaps Freudian, and it was Adam I was longing - Duh!). The feeling came and faded, but still no regrets.

Two weeks ago, as a tropical storm threatened Long Island, I decided to take Jude and his cousin Peter on our annual Love Lane visit. As we got closer, the winds picked up and a storm hit. It had been underestimated (at least by typically overreactive weather media standards). The winds were strong and I felt anxious driving along a tall-tree-sided main road. The rains poured down very briefly and my phone screamed a piercing tornado warning as we ran into the store. Unfazed, the kids got their bags and began to fill them with candy. I loved watching them go at it without any sobering preannounced limit. I like to think how Adam would have liked it and purposefully let them just go for it. I started to look around the store for myself. They still had the shiny bracelets, including one with "You Are My Sunshine." How nice? I decided to buy it and, of course, some candy for myself.

For some reason, it just wasn't the same. The candy was great, but I've worn the bracelet for the last two weeks, and it just didn't inspire the same connection. It felt forced, but I've kept it on anyway. I figured I'll wear it for a few weeks each year around his birthday. It was a great message for me, so cute and clever. So Adam.

Yesterday, I found myself alone with my mom in Westhampton. I was not lonely. I've spent a wonderful week with some of my kids, my brother Paul and his family, and my mom, Kitty. She and I stayed, and everyone else decided to go back Sunday for work and/or friends. I was planning to stay until Monday and have a few close beach friends over for wine to celebrate Adam. This year, the third year since his death, I haven't experienced the same sadness around his birthday as I did the first two. I was content. It was a no-beach rainy day, so I decided to take a ride to Love Lane and invited my mom. A perfect way to pass a wet "day before his birthday" day. When we got there, I went to the candy first: Pop rocks and ten pieces of dark chocolate molasses sponge, my usual. My mom got two big peppermint patties. While she was looking around, I walked over just to look at the shiny bracelets. The first one in the top left corner where my eyes naturally started, said,

"P.S. I Love You".

It was from him! It was, absolutely, Adam, I felt him chuckle self-satisfyingly and raise his eyes in feigned exasperation.

What I must do for you!! It's interesting how when I feel his presence I can hear him too. I can remember his chuckle or deep voice, and it sticks with me. Yes, this was the one from him. I almost felt nervous as I picked it up and noticed my hand shaking with emotion. His presence was so real.

… But I already had one. Did I really need two? Maybe I could give "You are My Sunshine" away again. Maybe I could give it to my mom since she was with me. Ohhh! What to do? It felt wasteful. Was it practical to keep shelling out $15 for cheap bracelets? Unsure, I took it anyway, just so no one else could buy it while I processed my decision. It didn't take much. What the heck? His birthday comes once a year. Yup, I needed it.

I noticed that the woman ringing me up was actually wearing the same t-shirt I had gotten as the gift for myself and Kit, last year. For some reason, as she was ringing up our stuff, I decided to share the story of why we were there and last year's bracelet. She got emotional. We all did. (I thought it was about me and Adam.) With tears in all of our eyes, she asked to see last year's bracelet, since she had already boxed up this new one. I showed it to her.

"You Are my Sunshine!" Wow! My brother passed away too, four years ago, and that was the song we played at his funeral. It has always been my thing for him. My brother was Frank McBride. She shared his name as if I might recognize it. I assumed there was a story. Instinctually, I took off the bracelet and handed it to her.

"Here, I think this is meant for you. Please take it; it's definitely for you."

She tried to politely refuse, but it had to be. It was from Adam and was clearly also from Frank. She could not refuse it. I drove away with one bracelet. One beautiful shiny bracelet from Adam that I absolutely LOVE. And she had hers from her brother. As we drove on toward the winery, Adam's presence was so strong. But he wasn't alone. I experienced the two of them - Adam and Frank McBride, high-fiving and laughing, filled with joy. "We did it!"

When I got home I googled "Frank McBride." It turned out there was a story. Frank McBride also died too young, and suddenly. He was only 34, a firefighter, hit by a train on his way home for lunch one day. A fluke, a sudden unexpected life-ending fluke. Just like Adam. ... And yet, that afternoon, two boys, these two young men whose lives had seemingly been snuffed out too young, seemed, actually, to be living it up!

What an incredible birthday gift!

Bright Sunshine

December 25, 2020

I'm sitting here today alone. It's Christmas, and Jude and Johnny have Covid. I've sent them to Westhampton, so that we can all quarantine without them infecting me. As I sit here reflecting on the past three years, I'm amazed, and I'm actually happy. Life is hard. My husband is still sick and I still have not seen him due to the Covid restrictions at his facility. He's declined horribly and I don't know what to expect when I see him for the first time, but who knows when that will be? I still have teenagers and 20-somethings who are figuring out their lives. They leave messes and have parties when I'm away. I am supposed to be on vacation next week and just found out I will be writing a report I overlooked. I just got a letter about a malfunction on my cardiac device. ...

Three years ago, take away the dead son, most of it would have been similar. But something critical has changed. Most of my life I suffered from an overshadowing sadness, a low-grade depression. People who know me experience a pretty upbeat person, but I was always sad and unsettled underneath, anxious, plagued by "what if's" and "if only's." I experienced pain about the past, worry about the future, and a longing for "better times." Easily fixated, I was consumed with the current problems, and often so caught up in "issues" that I missed everything else. I somehow let myself be too easily distracted from all the good, my blessings.

Something happened in the hospital that night as I said goodbye to Adam, when all those Thank you's gushed forth, as I saw the good his life had bestowed on mine, and was so genuinely grateful that I didn't even absorb the tragedy. Somehow, in the midst of this excruciating journey over these years, my ability to notice has continued to develop. All of the stories I've shared really occurred, I registered them, or sometimes they were pointed out to me, and even in my devastating sadness (please don't interpret anything I have written to downplay the bottomless sorrow and pain) they brought me joy. And I began to notice that too.

I was very angry with Adam when I first learned of the words he shared with JohnPaul a week before he died, "If I die I don't want anyone to be sad." I thought, "Yeah, sure. That's easy for a 15-year-old to say, you dumb f*&#!" On my drives home from work the first 18 months, I would cry and yell. I compartmentalized well. When I was at work, I worked. At home, I looked after the kids, tried my best to maintain all our lives, take care of Doug, and keep things positive. (I wasn't always successful, but gave my all.) In the car, though, I cried and cursed God. And when I wasn't screaming at God for being so mean, I yelled at Adam, "You are so stupid and naive. I hate you for ever saying that!!

But here I am now, and yes, he was right. Damn, he was always right! Since his death I have experienced the depths of horror. However, I have also been blessed with the recognition and awareness of these lights, and more and more I have been able to shift the balance of my attention. Yes, my husband is sick, but he shucked so many oysters for me in his life and he gave me this beautiful family. Yes, my kids are still figuring life out, but each one of them is individually awesome, I love when they are around, and my heart burns with their love. Yes, it was hard to see Adam's friends go off to college, but, wow! Mindy is at college. College!

Recently, a friend asked, "How are the kids?" My response was, "They are all great. And I see it." I used to get lost in my worry over their aches, struggles, health issues, etc. Lately I'm focused on how much I love them and what a wonderful life we have together. Problems still exist. I still hurt when my kids experience pain. But what's come into sharper focus is the joy each one of them brings me. Our relationships have lost the "cloud of concern" that can taint parent/child relationships. Yes, they are human. Sometimes way too teen and twenties human. But I even thank God for that, because they are *my* humans: handsome and beautiful, kind, with strong family values, and a deep love, and even like, for each other. Life is good!

~

We tend to be myopic. As a culture, society, even world, we have a tough time seeing beyond our own current and personal realities. Most of us, though, are familiar enough with somewhat recent world history to know, at least objectively, that, despite a pandemic, this is not the first time humanity has been in such a gloomy place, even if it is the darkest we remember. Many can recall 9/11; but, just beyond the memories of most of us alive today, there is also the Great Depression, a more deadly flu epidemic, World Wars, the Holocaust, and an endless list as you move further back through time.

Dark and hopeless periods are not new. The widespread deaths of young generations of men, due to hate, violence, and desire for power, occurred twice in World Wars in the previous century. During the Flu Epidemic of 1918, up to a third of the population was affected, and over 50 million people worldwide died. Just to put it in perspective, around 2 million people have died thus far due to Covid. The Great Depression lasted most of the 1930s, marked by individual and collective economic ruin, suicide, people hungry and displaced, and according to historians, unemployment rates over 20%. At the time I am writing now, the unemployment rate in the US remains elevated at about 7% due to Covid. "Racial cleansing" is far too benign a phrase for the gravity of collective evil and hate represented in the eradication of two thirds of the Jewish population in Europe during the Holocaust. The list, unfortunately goes on. Yes, humanity has done "dark," we have been here before, and far worse. We actually still carry it in our genes, within the memories and lives of our ancestors.

This narrative is drawn from and structured around a visitation sign-in book at a young boy's tragic death, a beautiful book of messages that generated themes, things about Adam that were perceived by others and memorable, and seemed to make the world a little brighter: "Adam's Hashtags for Living Yeezy." In my informal thematic analysis, I included only the qualities that people noticed in him, but there was something more in the data that was also quite inspiring, important, and very timely. In fact, the most frequent theme in the entire book was not about Adam, or one of his traits. It was something that came from the kids themselves, and was directed at him, or more frequently us, his family, in pain. It was Love.

There were 68 emoji ♥s and the word "love" was used over 160 times, "Love" directed at Adam, or showered on us, all because of his death - a tsunami of love (what else do you call two five-hour stretches of visitation lines of people waiting to give us hugs or fat-lip-from-shoulder-pad embraces?) generated by a personally earthshaking tragedy. This is especially important to highlight now, in a world where things aren't going so well, and so many have lost hope.

Yes, there's more to the story, important to keep in mind in our present circumstances. In much the same way that this powerful love, new friendships, and so many other blessings presented in the midst of (or resulting from) our terrible tragedy, ill-fated chapters in history also tend to be followed by periods of hope and renewal, times of light, a new day.

The Roaring Twenties followed the flu of 1918, and was marked by a period of economic growth and innovation, and young people having a lot of fun. Post-World War II America was marked by great and widespread economic expansion, first stages of focus on women's and minority rights, and a baby boom which would create the wealthiest generation in U.S. history. Even in the wake of the darkest despairs of the Holocaust, without diminishing the true evil, there are incredible stories of hope, resilience, love, heroism, and sacrifice, and even blessings after.

In most of these scenarios, it was the young generation who carried the torch through the transformation. They brought their hope, energy, aspiration, perseverance, generosity, and authenticity. In much the same way the kids showed up for us, it was the young adults who ushered in those tomorrows, and uncovered hope from the bleak and stagnant malaise.

For me personally, it took sitting down to write about the dreams, stories, signs and experiences around Adam's life and death, to be inspired to a new, if obvious, awareness, that out of darkness comes light; out of winter, spring; that dawn follows the night; and that Hope and Joy often follow a similar pattern.

In each of the individual stories, there were "Lights," even strong focused beams, consistently highlighting pathways towards my own Peace and Joy. They resonated hope, truth, spiritual presence, individual human dignity, authenticity, and simple gratitude. Fortunately, to make it obvious and special (at least for this reluctant learner, his own heartbroken mother), Adam's lights were often accompanied by his very distinct and comforting presence. There were times I laughed out loud feeling his exasperation over the deliberate and conspicuous efforts required for him to get through to me. Even more amazing was the fact that each time I sat to write a story, the message that came through seemed to connect so much to now. The messages in the memories, dreams, stories of his life and things that happened in the wake of it, each seemed to highlight something important and germane to the current events.

Needless to say, a narrative about experiences related to a child's sudden unexpected death will have its share of pain and darkness. It was necessary, as well as real and appropriate to begin with that. (Let's face it, since Covid shut down our world in March 2020 things have been pretty tough too.) As I wrote throughout this time, there were instances where the visceral re-experience brought objectivity, and a first real awareness of the incredible horror of it all. Some days I was drained and in physical pain after, only to walk away and see the riots and cities burning on TV. My neck and shoulders hurt most of the summer and I regularly walked into town for back and neck massages - something I had never done previously.

But it was also in the midst of this new objective awareness of tragedy, this first non-surreal encounter, that the visible contrast became so evident. I gained a new awareness and perceptions of the stories and experiences I was writing about. I was able to recognize the "Lights" and their accompanying love, and to make connections to these times in which we live.

And so, here I am, months later, after hundreds of written, saved, and discarded pages, many massages, rivers of tears, and lightbulb moments of awareness. I'm still a mom who lost her young precious child continuing to endure the forever aches and sadness, and the actual physical hole. I still cry when precious pictures pop up on the digital frame in my kitchen. I feel the pain of his absence in family gatherings and important dates that would have been milestones. I fight a cloud over my kitchen table on random regular evenings, or when I make a new exciting friend who will never know him. But I am newly able to exist in, and more importantly, be aware of, the contrast; and I have come to a real and genuine acceptance. I have found peace and discovered joy I never possessed. Adam's presence is actually more vivid and real to me now, in some ways more than when he was alive, and I communicate with him regularly. As crazy as it may sound, I have come to an acceptance that his life, even its brevity, had a purpose. I can actually "smile because it happened."

So, in these pages I've tried to share that. Most especially, this is written for young people - his brothers and sisters, cousins, friends; those who had drifted apart before his death; those who may have known of him even if they were not close; and those who never met or even heard of him too.

You guys are our Hope. While my generation has tangled ourselves up in the complex systems that were supposed to make things better, gotten consumed in toxic and angry social media, buried under the pressures of accumulating or maintaining our wealth or power, managing our careers, investments or properties, surviving, smothered in unhealthy relationships, or even trying to make it better for our kids, you guys are still unencumbered and free - you don't have all our baggage. You are still uncalloused, untainted, more closely connected with what is real, righteous, and authentic. You are still fresh, light, and free enough to choose your paths and the roads you will follow to the place you want to be. You can create the world you envision and are still blessed with the capacity for hope, that many my age lost, probably sometime in our thirties.

Unlike many today, I'm heartened thinking about the future. I like imagining a world driven by the values of the young people I have met and gotten to know through Adam (my lights from the darkness), as well as my own beautiful children, Adam's siblings. Perhaps what is most telling and amazing of all, is that all of this came during such angst ridden and unsettling times – and during Covid, when I sat down to write in the spring because things were shut down and I finally had the time. I hope that in sharing these lights Adam has let flicker for me, you might be reinforced and further inspired.

In August, on Adam's birthday and after my wonderful day on the North Fork, and a nice night with friends commemorating his birthday, I found myself alone in the cottage unready for bed. I was so happy after my day that I decided to sit and listen to music, and enjoy my shiny new "P.S. I Love You" bracelet that had been making me smile all afternoon and evening. I lit a candle in the quiet kitchen, opened a beer, and put on a Spotify 70's playlist.

Once again, I felt his presence in the music. And then, "I Can See Clearly Now the Rain is Gone" by Johnny Nash came on. Not a new song at all; it had never been a favorite, or anything I connected with before, but now it resonated. It was totally new and all for me. I was connected to Adam. It was clearly from him, from the very first line I knew we had a new song. Like before, this was a family affair. My brother Brian was singing and my Dad seamlessly navigated the differing tones on an electric piano. Adam and I were dancing in sync. He twirled and spun me in his perfectly cool, contained, and happy, "If I die, don't be sad" rhythm.

And I realized the rain really is gone.

Yes, now the sun shines more brightly, most importantly, I notice and love it! Adam, thank you. I'm sorry for all the rants and cursing. My kids have always been patient with me, and it appears you were right after all.

We all encounter darkness, the trick is to be mindful, keep your eyes open and don't miss out on the lights.

#AdamsWorld

Epilogue: I'm here, Mom!

"Mom, where's Adam?"
The unforeseen unknowingly epochal question

Piercing a groggy cloud ...
the moment - so singular and defining -
breaks through dull unexpecting sleepy fog.

Where's Adam?
Concern rises, angst develops,
The frantic dog at the door without him ...
        gut feelings
        adrenaline rising

ADAM! NOOO!
The piercing scream of his brother gone looking,
ADAAAAAM!
Loud, bloodcurdling, dynamic energy-filled screams,
Desperate,
"ADAM! NOOOOOO!"
Adrenaline takes over.

His sick looking body there on the curb,
        lifeless?
Stepping back I become an observer
Aware but unfeeling
What's happened?
Oh! My God! What's wrong?
        dead or alive?
My God! Where's Adam?

I'm here, Mom,
In the love of my brother who works to revive me,
and the neighbors who surround us,
my friend encouraging me to be ok.
In the strength that overtakes you,
In your awareness of the pain of the mom
looking on in the distance,
In the empathy of those on the scene,
In your calm ...

It's me, Adam. I'm here.

Memory fails of the ride in the police car
numbness is all I recall,
I don't even know if I knew
It still torments

I'm here in my brother's calm strength.

The hectic ER, doctors, professionals
but no one connected
Our incredible crisis
separated and anonymous
stares from patients and families
relegated to chairs away from the reality
so far from my boy
Where's Adam?

I'm here, Mom,
In the love of the friends who come to you
In the sustaining bond holding you and Johnny
I'm here in your strength directing the chaos

In your resolute direction to the doctor
In your brave command
I'm here in her reminder to find a priest
        in the priest not being there
        your privilege to bless and send me.
I'm in the strength and manliness you sense as you hold me
        though my body is lifeless
In the heart filled Thank yous of your farewell
        ... instead of regrets
In the Joy and Love that you will remember and feel
        ... instead of sadness
I'm here as you put me in the arms of strong angels
        as you watch them take me
        place me in comforting Motherly arms
In your Peace and contentment
It's me, Adam. I'm here.

We are left in the driveway
But an unknown place.
What is the next step
        when it's so unnatural to move forward?
His brother there in the headlights
        expectant, for different news,
"He didn't make it. I'm sorry. He's gone."
His disbelief and torment
My God, how can this be?

I'm here, in your control delivering crushing news
and the gentle presence of his friend

The long first night,
our house and hearth cold and empty,
as if they need to be sure I know.
The clock stands still
       but moves too fast
each passing minute further distances us
       closer to tomorrow night,
       ...And every night after
The threat of bed, alone with my torment.
There are no guidelines,
Nothing to say,
So we sit.

In the comfort of the friends who connect and show up.
       In your brother, in your niece, in your mom,
       The call from the plane,
       In the love of my family,
In the firewood at dawn, escorted by warmth
       the fire that burns for days
       The love that brought it
And the love in the masses who descend

I'm here.
I was never gone, Mom!
It's me, Adam,
I'm here, Mom!
Always

Acknowledgments:

Like any good kid, I'll start with mom. Mine in particular deserves extra. Thank you, Kitty, for being my ongoing editor and sounding board at every stage. Thanks for the glasses of wine and the impromptu, "You know what? I'm just going to make dinner for you guys tonight." For being there through the development of this emotional manuscript, and every other time of need - and joy! And most of all, for instilling my strong faith which, when it comes down to it, is what made my process of healing and discovery, and this book, possible in the first place. You're the best mom ever. It's that simple.

To Billy, Kit, Mindy, JohnPaul, and Jude, I am so blessed by our love. What we have endured together I wouldn't wish on anyone, but I also wouldn't trade out an ounce of what we now possess as a family. I feel so lucky to have you all, and know that you each continue to share Adam's special spirit in this world.

There are two people in particular who enabled this to happen, Sally Richardson and Laura Savard. Sally, your friendly gentle smile on the beach, offered generously for so many years prior, enabled me to take the risk and approach you with my first stab at this last summer. No matter what I write here it will not fairly represent the impact you have had on this important chapter in my life. Thank you for your ongoing guidance over this past year and for your honest (but always kind first) feedback. You are my Covid silver lining as well!

Laura, thank you for taking such a genuine interest in learning more of our story after filling a special role in our family's well-being and recovery. I kept promising you I would write to fill in the details, and here it is finally!

Thank you to my editors, Hannah Howard and Elaine Porter. You each played a critical role in getting this to where I'm proud it's gotten. Though you both came through my network of friendship - my affinity for the personal - your professional expertise helped facilitate something beyond my own amateurity! Thanks also to Joel Fotinos. We have never even met, but your generosity in sharing very thoughtful, sensitive and detailed insights is so appreciated. Your guidance in the email Sally forwarded was the beacon I kept returning to.

Dan Paggoli, your talents with a camera and software turn a frame into art.

Ray Rice, Gina Ruggiero and Rashad Cherry, we are going to change the world together. Thank you!

To my thought team: Fr. Thomas Petrillo, Corey Baron, Tim Vallierre, Jennifer Russo, Rachel Howard, Stephanie Bellantoni, and Katherine Nicholls. Each one of you offered unique and direction-changing insight and helped make this better. Your input enabled the transformation of this manuscript from something I felt good about into a finished work that brings me joy.

And finally, thank you Adam, for being here when I really need you, and for patiently and persistently bringing light to the lights.

Thank you, I love you all.

About the Author:

Naomi Brickel, is a mom of six children (one in heaven) and resides in New Rochelle, NY where all of her kids attend or graduated from the public schools. She has spent her adult life dedicated to raising her large family, volunteering in her community, and a career in non-profit service. In her work she has helped families in the practical and emotional aspects of navigating disability service systems across the lifespan, building capacity with professionals for more inclusive programming, and working with individuals themselves to promote their self-determination and empowerment.

Naomi's resonating happiness is rooted in her newfound awareness of the loving energy driving existence and of the individual light and dignity of each person she encounters - lessons she learned in the process of grieving the sudden death of her blessed son Adam.

Inspired?

Adam's life was noted for simple yet impactful acts of acceptance, outreach, and kindness. Author, Naomi Brickel, former NFL star, Ray Rice, community volunteer, Gina Ruierro, and Rashad Cherry, founder and owner of Amoúr, a high-end New Rochelle based streetwear brand, have come together to develop a merchandise store inspired by themes generated from the stories of Adam's life.

#Adam'sWorld will carry on Adam's legacy by supporting those who could use an extra hand on their shoulder. For more information visit www.naomibrickel.com

~

*If you enjoyed reading **Not to Spoil the Ending...** please consider inspiring others to do the same by leaving a review on our amazon page!*

Made in United States
North Haven, CT
31 October 2021